He Will Guide You

He Will Guide You

Truth, Experience The Holy Spirit

By Rev. Dr. John Diomede

Xulon Elite

Xulon Press Elite
2301 Lucien Way #415
Maitland, FL 32751
407.339.4217
www.xulonpress.com

Scripture quotations taken from the Holy Bible, New International Version (NIV). Copyright © 1973, 1978, 1984, 2011 by Biblica, Inc.™. Used by permission. All rights reserved.

Edited by Xulon Press.

Printed in the United States of America.

ISBN-13: 9781545611920

ACKNOWLEDGEMENTS/DEDICATIONS

To My God
Who helps me hear His Holy Spirit and gave me the following
relationships

To Maryann
My Wife
Who helps me understand the
process of life

To John, Joseph, Christopher, Steven, David
My Sons
Who help me understand the reality of life

To Bill Fritzky
My Friend
Who helps me understand the charity of life

Table of Contents

ARE YOU LISTENING?

Introduction

T his is a book about the potential relationship between God and the individual human being. This is of vital importance for success in a Kingdom that will never end. Jesus made it very clear that hearing the voice of the Holy Spirit was a promise from Him and the Father; it would be the norm for one's life. This book attempts to bring insight into that relationship. It also clarifies the direction of His voice in terms of application and result for life's actions of a Kingdom citizen. My desire is simply to offer information on the critical necessity of hearing and responding to God's voice. Here are some thoughts to consider as you move through this book.

Do we know what hearing and listening are? Jesus said, "He who has ears, let him hear." I will offer thoughts on this everyday activity. We hear in many different ways and often take for granted this simple process. Those of us whose hearing organs function properly sometimes don't fully consider the designed process of hearing. Yes, hearing is much more than hearing, if you get my drift. So, hearing what's important in life is a matter of caring, listening, understanding, and knowing the filters we employ. Hearing God through His Holy Spirit uses all of this and more. Yes, He even uses physical experiential sensations in the communication of truth. This is part of the hearing process. The challenges that we face in hearing the voice of the Holy Spirit are significant. Human brokenness, the world, and the spiritual enemy are culprits that drown out God the Holy Spirit's voice. We will examine these closely as we stretch out to touch and open up to receive the God of the Bible. If we can learn to hear regularly, it helps us to make decisions with a proper attitude—the attitude of submission. Submitting to God is of supreme value; we must hear Him to submit to Him

One last note before we get started: you will encounter the word *broken* throughout this writing. The clear majority, if not all, of the intended applications should be interpreted like a cracked mirror or a car that is missing a wheel. In other words, "something that does not function as originally designed."

Standard, Regulation, Principle, Code

These words speak of a level of measure, quality, and attainment for one's life. Often, they are applied as a form of definition or to give identity. With so much noise all around us each day—at home, on the job, or in public—how can we determine if we have a high level of good decision-making if we are unable to filter out the meaningless distractions and heed what really matters? What do you listen to and for, and how does what you hear impact your life?

As I write these words, the United States comes to mind. We live in a time when a battle is raging. Our country is on the cusp of realization that the battle raging within is between two factions: one with a desire to preserve what was established at its inception versus the desire to alter that foundation. Of course, interpretation is valuable, but as you will see later, both sides can present valid arguments that make the other sound radical. The standard is changing because both groups hear two different messages from the same foundational documents. Unfortunately, we do not have those authors here to define their original words. Would it not be helpful if they could communicate to us today? Politicians, both liberal and conservative, and the judiciary have been the organizational interpreters for centuries. They have been guilty of manipulating the message of this governing standard established by their earliest predecessors. The early standard was determined at great cost. In the film *The Patriot,* just before the start of the Revolutionary War, the main character, Benjamin Martin, who is played by Mel Gibson, says:

But mark my words. This war will be fought not on the frontier or on some distant battlefield, but amongst us—among our homes. Our children will learn of it with their own eyes. . . . [1]

The standards of the United States were developed by individuals who wanted to protect this land from tyranny and war. They made the Constitution the best they could. Their foundational documents, like the Bible, are open to interpretation by broken humans: broken people writing broken messages to broken recipients to prevent them from repeating human struggles. But brokenness leads to struggles, and war is ugly, even philosophical and theological wars, the war of words. As the father of two military sons, I can share the challenges that come with the clamorous thief of physical war. In some cases, it takes lives, but in all cases war steals something of greater value. The most troubling is loss of self and innocence, leaving wounds that cannot be seen or bandaged.

Today, our government or "ruling family" is insulated by money and corruption. The war they fight is this war of words and rhetoric through the maneuverings of public media. The grand halls of our political establishments provide not only insulation but an amnesic that makes the individuals who walk them forget the horror and the unseen because it is not their children's eyes who have seen physical war on our homeland. But they are seeing the spark of philosophical war. They are individuals whose decision-making brings on hate, violence, and destruction because they don't realize that they have access to hearing God through His Holy Spirit.

Discernment is more about hearing than seeing. The deafness that consumes conscience does not hold our leaders accountable, and even the few who may survive that conscience consumption are caught in a web so complex that it is fatiguing to ponder. Our judicial system is so politicized that it cannot even dispense the healing treatment of justice for the people. Thus, the standard is disintegrating because the political leadership can see but cannot hear the people. In some cases, it is a downright refusal to establish a connective relationship. There are so many special interests that no one is interested in the holistic life of the organism—one nation for all. This is not simply a result of blindness or delusion. It is a choice. It answers the question, "What is best for me as an individual, exclusive of others who share our soil and laws?"

The new standard on all levels is "me." A comedian, Brian Reagan, refers to this all-encompassing selfhood as "the me monster." It is funny because it is true. We laugh at our brokenness because we don't know how to fix it. This country, this Constitution, has come down to each individual deciding what the standard is for every situation. Unlike the mothers who centuries ago threw their children over the wall onto the swords of the attacking army, fear of our own existence is not so obvious, so we can tritely adopt decision-making without one prevailing standard. We have reality shows, singing and dancing shows, Facebook, Twitter, and much more wherein the values we once held dear as a society are now held up to ridicule. These entertainment media allow us to become callous to the society we live in because as Magneto, the famous X-Men bad guy, says, "Once again, it's all about you![2]

Government's corrupt standard operating procedure has also come to define the organizational units that claim to be part of the "organization" of the Messiah, Jesus. Yes, I am referring to the Kingdom of God. Like the organization of government, the organization of the church does not represent the Kingdom of God. It cannot. Messiah's Kingdom is within the individual. The touch-point is the presence of and communication with the Holy Spirit within each accepting heart.

Standards of "leaders" should not define God's people, not when they contradict the standards established by God. Holy standards direct us to love our neighbors as ourselves. Those who accept God's standard choose to live with compassion and mercy that enter and reside in their souls through hearing the Holy Spirit— compassion and mercy for all, not just those of their choosing. Jesus asked, "What good is loving those who already love you?" When we listen and hear God's voice, we begin to understand His standard in a personal way. It supersedes the voice of rote religion and structured organization. It speaks in the moment and relates to making a decision in time. It is like having an epiphany at your disposal at any time.

I have come to love the voice of the Holy Spirit because He has challenged my way of thinking. He breaks me down to acknowledge the nothing that I am who can become something through the grace of God. Remember this saying: "If you want to win, you need to lose!" Jesus said it this way, "If you want to find your life here, you must lose it." Your choices for your life collide with God's choices, and those moments are not emanating from outside but from a relationship with Him who chooses to dwell with you, in your house. How can you get to know someone unless you spend time together? As you get acquainted with the Holy Spirit in a deeper way, He will speak your language. He will use circumstances in your life in which to communicate and have relationship with you. He will find you, and you will know it.

How the Bible Speaks to Us

The Bible is a language guide. Most people who have given themselves serious exposure to the Bible generally agree it could be made to say anything. It can also support a plethora of opposing viewpoints. By design, it is controversial, fragmented, and outside of its writers' personal views, inconclusive to some of the most important matters concerning God. This is not an error. The design of God was to allow humans to write about their relationship with Him. Other people could learn from that relationship, especially the concept that they, too, could have a similar relationship to those modeled in His Word. This personal, individual relationship must be birthed, incubated, grown, and matured. The challenge is that it's difficult to relate one human experience to another because we humans are "alone," a topic I will elaborate on in a later chapter. Biblical relational manifestation occurs within the writer, and more importantly, within each of us, and is based on one's commitment to the voice that moves them to act, speak, or write at the moment they hear. An example of this voice is found in these two Bible verses:

Before I formed you in the womb I knew you, And before you were born I consecrated you; I have appointed you a prophet to the nations." (Jeremiah 1:5 NASB)

5

And,

> And John bore witness saying, "I have seen the Spirit descending as a dove out of heaven, and He remained upon Him. "And I did not recognize Him, but He who sent me to baptize in water said to me, "The One upon whom you see the Spirit descending and remaining upon Him, He is the one who baptizes in the Holy Spirit." (John 1:32–33 MW)

The voice these individuals heard is the voice of the Holy Spirit. He speaks to those who wish to listen and even more to those who desire to listen. You must be ready to hear Him—to seek Him, even. But that path means you will likely have to wait for His voice. You must be patient, and you must brace yourself for He speaks truth. You will know truth because it is not cognitive knowledge; it is experiential. When He speaks, you will listen because you want to and because it is the most important thing you will ever hear—you will know this intuitively. The voice will begin to change you before you can be used as a conduit to help others change, and the path will be similar to all who seek Him and yet be experienced independently by each believer.

But how can we be sure of correctly identifying the voice of the Holy Spirit? This stems from concern over the problem of biblical ownership. In other words, whose interpretation is correct? Over the past 2,000 years, misguided people have committed horrible acts in the name of biblical interpretation and the voice of God. Which person or group can accurately offer valid biblical interpretation? This question presents a dilemma, thus, the general population has sidelined the Bible as necessary reading, while allowing their respective faith-based organizations to direct them in the analysis, understanding, and explanation of its content. Various denominations convert text into doctrinal theology that their adherents simply accept without question as presented by their leaders. The concept of faith, belief, or trust then becomes incorporated into doctrine, which is then layered upon and controlled by other doctrines of those organizations. This process leads not to a deeper trust relationship with God, but to a shelving of the book that points the individual toward a personal relationship with the Holy Spirit, the discovery of Jesus the Messiah, and eternal life.

True seekers must take ownership of this book and face its challenges head on, in a personal way. They must challenge every conclusion offered by a so-called "expert" and every principle that they have been taught about this book by the "experts" until faith through relationship with the Holy Spirit begins to cause a relationship that stirs confidence, inspiring them toward self-change that manifests in a life of ever-growing compassion for others. Compassion is the key because compassion always expresses itself in action. Like biblical writers, if the desire to know God is important enough, one must seek the relationship of which this book testifies. No one can have relationship void of contact, communication, and a desire to know the one true God—the Creator of the universe. This is what the writers desired and experienced. They were no different than you and me. Their road contained the same potholes, hills, bumps, curves, and forks that ours does.

> But apart from faith it is impossible to please *Him,* for it is necessary for the one who comes to God believes that He exists, and *that* He is a rewarder of those who seek Him. (Hebrews 11:6 MW)

Listening for the communication of the Bible—through physical hearing of the Word being read aloud or spiritual hearing through silent reading—teaches us that God speaks to individual people, people like you and me. The Bible is an impetus to each of us to be confident that you are known and not alone.

In the battles being fought today, the only real refuge we have or need is responding to God's Word as communicated through the still, small voice of the Holy Spirit when we find ourselves ready to listen.

WHOSE VOICE DO YOU HEAR?

Hear, Listen, Understand, Care

Jesus said, "Those who have ears, let them hear." Is hearing simply a function of an organ of the human body? We know that this is not accurate because there are many people whose hearing ability has been compromised. We also know that hearing is very different than listening, which is also different than understanding, which is still different from caring.

In our home, my sons' bedrooms were one level up from the main living level and my wife's and my bedroom. When there was a family gathering at another location, we needed to get in the car when it was time to leave, and I needed to get their attention. I would call up to them, "Time to go!" I know that they heard me, yet sometimes there was no response. A few minutes would pass, and I would call out again to them. They might call back to me, saying, "Okay, Dad; we will be right down."

Now, they were now listening. But minutes would tick by, and maybe one or two of the boys would appear, but a communication problem persisted with the rest.

I would walk over to the stairwell, point my head upward in their direction, raise my voice, and call again. One of the remaining three would come running down the stairs. He understood.

After about ten seconds, I would begin my ascent up the stairs. This was evidenced by my wedding band clinking on the wrought iron railing, a sound that I was not aware of for a long time, but my sons were aware of it. The two last bodies came flying down the steps so fast that they nearly knocked me over—now they finally cared!

During this time, as my sons were in their rooms, there were five voices all yapping, clamoring, arguing, and laughing. One by one each, in his own time, heard more clearly, culminating with the last hearing not by words but by nonverbal communication. The last ones could not hear until they actually heard, if you catch my drift.

For each of us, there are only four voices to be heard: The voice of self, the voice of the world, the voice of the enemy, and the voice of God. Earlier, I mentioned Magento saying mockingly, "It is all about you." This is the voice of the world. It actually claims that life is not about you; it is about the "not you" component of life. It is rhetorical, sarcastic. The voice of the world is like a line from the film *Matrix* when Morpheus speaks:

> The Matrix is a system, Neo. That system is our enemy. But when you're inside, you look around, what do you see? Businessmen, teachers, lawyers, carpenters. The very minds of the people we are trying to save. . . . The Matrix is the world that has been pulled over your eyes to blind you from the truth.[3]

The world's voice comprises the normal, everyday things we encounter. It is your boss saying, "Good job." It is your neighbor complaining about taxes. It is the media encouraging you to be suspicious of everything. It is the messages in your inbox and comments on Facebook. It is the unending stream of voices endlessly filling your mind in an attempt to block out the voice of the Holy Spirit—the only voice worth hearing. This world will try to take you away from making an effort to read your Bible and distract you from learning the language of "you"—the only language God speaks when addressing you. We will talk more about the voice of the world later, but we can generally understand the pervasive nature of everyday sounds and voices that distract us from what is truly important—the voice of God. The world in all its glory and agony is the biggest obstacle that prevents us from recognizing truth, it has been pulled over our eyes.

Self-Talk

There came a time in my life that I realized, as far as my humanity is concerned, I was alone. Yes, I have a wonderful family, friends, and acquaintances, but it does not change what I know to be true. I don't like the idea of being alone, nor do I espouse it. The problem is that this aloneness is a truth I cannot get away from. As a pharmacist, I have dispensed tens of thousands of pills to help people cure their aloneness. Before I go on, please understand that the following statements will bring us in range of the border of the physical and metaphysical, the soul and its visibility. Science has concluded that depression, along with a host of other diagnoses, such as lack of sleep, stem from a chemical in our brain known as serotonin. Humans diagnosed with these types of conditions usually have low serotonin levels in the brain. Serotonin, in medical circles, is known as our "happy" chemical. The closer we are to having normal or above-normal levels of serotonin, the happier we are and the better we sleep, think, and deal with life. In other words, with adequate serotonin, we seem less broken.

Science says stress is the enemy of serotonin. We live in a world that is endemic with stress and, I don't have to tell you, it is getting worse. A vast number of people are popping selective serotonin reuptake inhibitors (SSRIs) like candy in order to get levels up because medical science has concluded that these pills help humans. But the epidemic only gets worse day by day. More and more prescription drugs are being used to cure what ails us emotionally. Unfortunately, they may only provide temporary relief because the real problem that ails us is aloneness.

I went through a bout of depression twenty-five years ago. What I learned is the doctors and pharmacists cannot get into our head with us, so they send a chemical. Our family and friends cannot get into our heads with us, so their result is frustration, anger, sympathy, and a host of other emotions. Everyone is fighting this invisible foe. All are hurting and daily wondering how to beat this enemy. No one knows exactly _what_ another human feels. People can sympathize or empathize, but the gulf still exists, and no one can cross over. Dietrich Bonhoeffer, the Christian pastor, prophet, and martyr, noticed this almost a century ago:

> Only when a man sees that office is a penultimate (one level below the top) authority in the face of an ultimate (the top), indescribable authority, in the face of the authority of God, has the real situation been reached. And before this Authority the individual knows himself to be completely alone.[4]

Bonhoeffer saw a deep truth and made his point referencing, among other subjects, politics. But this truth also exists at the personal level: The "office" of individuality. When the individual realizes his or her humanity and individuality, there is a personal reckoning of sorts. And the reckoning is not momentary; it is daily. In our age of information, we now know that our heroes such as movie stars, athletes, the wealthy, and the powerful are all hurting. No one is immune from aloneness. Human weakness cannot be eliminated. It must be trumped by the desire to seek God and acknowledge our aloneness.

> For the creation was subjected to futility, not of its own will, but because of the One who subjected it, in hope that the creation itself also will be delivered from the bondage of decay into the liberty of the glory of the children of God. (Romans 8:20–21 MW)

In the above scripture, the individual acknowledges that we were subjected, by God, to losing, being alone in the hope that we would go to God. Jesus offers this for our aloneness:

> "And I will ask the Father, and He will give you another Advocate so that He may be with you forever- the Spirit of truth, whom the world cannot receive, because it neither sees Him nor knows Him. You know Him because He lives with you, and will be in you." (John 14:16–17 MW)

Except for free will, this is the greatest gift we have within our God-given resources. With our free will, we can call on Jesus and receive an answer that we can hear—the gift of the Holy Spirit. Jesus was never alone! Why? "And I knew that You (Father) hear Me always; but because of the people standing around I said it, that they may believe that You did send Me" (John 11:42 MW). Also: "And He who sent Me is with Me; He has not left Me alone, for I always do the things that are pleasing to Him" (John 8:29 MW).

Jesus was not plagued by the voice of self. It existed in Him, but he chose not to obey self. By free will, Jesus consciously chose his actions. He chose the Father over the world. He, like you and I, knew the fact of self. Yet, he chose others over self. He informed his close friends of his thoughts and what was coming. But from a human perspective, he could not bridge aloneness. Only the Holy Spirit could, and only Jesus could send Him. He knew there was a way inside people. He knew there was a voice that would pierce the vacuum of existence. Yes, there were indications of hope:

> Now when Jesus came into the region of Caesarea Philippi, He *questioned* His disciples, "Who do people say that the Son of Adam is?" They said, "Some *say* John the Baptist; and others, Elijah. And others, Jeremiah, or one of the prophets." He said to them, "But who do you say that I am?" Simon Peter answered, "You art the Messiah, the Son of the living God." Jesus responded to him, "There is good for you, Simon son of Jonah, because flesh and blood has not revealed *this* to you, but My Father who is in heaven." (Mathew 16:13–17 MW)

Peter experienced the only resolution to our aloneness that exists: the voice of God the Father, through the Holy Spirit. Receiving the Holy Spirit is the cure to being alone. He is not our conscience. He is not our mental conversations. He is a spiritual intuition of sorts that manifests in our souls. He is our friend, comforter, and advocate—if we choose. So, as the grail knight in *Indiana Jones and the Last Crusade* film said, "You must choose; choose wisely"[5]. How do we choose wisely? This process is challenging and time-consuming. If you know little of the Bible, this is the beginning of the learning process. If you "know the Bible," it will take you a bit longer because you must unlearn much of error-infused church teaching. To offer a comparable scenario, if Jesus, God Incarnate, walked daily denying Himself; if the Apostle Paul said, "Work out your salvation in fear and trembling"; then you and I have a long journey. If you are able to listen past the call of the world, your next obstacle to hearing God's voice is you.

You're Not the Boss of Me

Maryann and I have raised five sons. While each has a personality vastly different from his brothers, one was a "strong-willed child." They all had various degrees of influence on my growth as a parent and person—significant influence, all due to their differences. But Christopher caused me to search hard for answers. I am not sure where I first heard the statement, "You're not the boss of me.." I think it was a radio interview of an author on the topic, but it was very apropos for my son's situation. I saw it in his eyes, heard it in his voice, and recognized it in his actions.

Over the years, as I have learned more from the Holy Spirit, it has become evident that this phrase is not reserved for strong-willed children. It applies to all of us, and it is destructive. Yes, we want to be our own boss rather than follow the guidance of others. Earlier I mentioned four stages of comprehension: hearing, listening, understanding, and caring. It is hard to understand when one does not care, but it is impossible to listen when one does not hear.

When I was young in the Lord, I had quite a bit of trouble in worship services. Distraction became the norm. How someone looked, how someone sounded, how someone stood, dressed, and a host of other silly thoughts separated me from experiencing God as He wanted me to know Him. Just a few years ago, some twenty-five years into my journey, I began to enjoy music as a facet of worship freely. I started to understand that God is my boss because I began to care about what God cared about. He has instructed me, as I heard His voice, to use my free will, so I can be the boss of me in a constructive manner and direct my will to follow His. God does not overpower us to follow Him. God does not inhabit us to control us. God allows us to be the decision makers of our personal destinies. If we choose Him with a desire to understand we begin to listen. If we choose to follow His will in a caring way, then we can understand. When the last two of my sons ran down the stairs, understanding was reactionary. They did not really understand. True understanding came after those two cared, just like me. Religion does not make us care, understand, listen, or hear. Religion (a voice of the world) teaches us, "You're not my boss." This is why denominations cannot get together. They espouse their way, period. In the church at large I have encountered, and was part of, a pompous hardness which revealed itself with a smile, a caring tone, a sort of concern that faded away with the wants of the organization. You've experienced it; it is why so many people church hop. When God allows us access to Himself, we are humbled and may even be broken when we see everything through His eyes (this can be overwhelming). The more we access Him from a caring perspective, the more we can understand about hearing Him. The more we understand, the better decision makers we become. The better a decision maker you become, the more effectively you can hear His voice.

This morning, my son Joseph and I had a conversation about his critical thinking class and the word *pragmatic*. The question was, "How would you explain to someone the definition of the word *pragmatic?* It means *practical*. Critical thinking is not a task-oriented process; it is a means-oriented process. Figure out the means, and you can be pragmatic about anything. A relationship with God is means-oriented. The Holy Spirit offers the information for good decision-making that helps you to be the boss of your reality with God being your boss.

Habits, Decision-making, and God's Interest

As a pharmacist, I deal with patients who have various emotional conditions that manifest as addictions, compulsions, obsessions, and the like. Most medical professionals will agree the decision-making process in these individuals is overtly compromised. Let's call them habits for the sake of this section. If we consider the process of making a decision and how it occurs, we can drill down to a more obscure and hidden form of brokenness and compromised decision-making. I have free will, and I make many choices daily. For example, if I am thirsty, I drink; if I am lonely, I may fill the void with some type of contact—for example, television, social media, music, or people. When I am hungry, I eat. These are all mundane, normal decisions. The vast majority of people will agree that these decisions are not emblematic or even germane to hearing God's voice in any significant manner because God does not really care about these choices. But since God cares about people, I say He cares about their decisions because their decisions impact life. We will return to this thought later.

So, why is it that sometimes I eat even when I am not hungry? And sometimes I make many of the above choices when there is no need attached. I just watched the film *Hidden Figures* and witnessed a host of white people, male and female, make bad decisions concerning their treatment of black people. These white individuals would not consider themselves "bad" people. But, boy, were they bad decision-makers! Why is this? The reason is we are inclined to compulsion, a lack of self-control, and mob-like thinking, all of which wages war with our good decision-making ability we can have if we can hear the voice of God and if we know the difference between His voice and all others. The film characters simply could not make ethical decisions involving people of color. The voice of God brings boldness against what is wrong. The lack of His voice lends to cowardice and leads people to conclude that He is not interested in the minutia of our lives. An artistic work, such as a film, play, sculpture, or even music, attests to the brokenness of humanity and how other voices, the wrong voices, influence us to a bad decision-making process.

The voice of the world supports this thinking because it tells us we are thinking logically. Data, which too often replaces God, validates our mindset. This ignorance is rooted in our propensity to score behavior. The film depicted a time in our country's history when it was logical to be prejudiced because whites were assumed to be better at almost everything than blacks. Although this assumption is neither logical nor accurate, we bought into it as a country and a culture with dire consequences that we continue to experience today.

Addiction to illegal drugs is dramatically rising as a leading disruptor of normal life and moral values. But what about television, movies, computers, junk food, expensive cars and houses, flashy headlines, and controlling people? The list goes on. All of these "fillers" of our time speak to the lack of hearing or seeking of God. A recent potent addiction is social media. It may be the pinnacle of all addictions and potentially has a more profound effect on us than illegal drugs because, unlike opoids, it invisibly corrupts our decision-making process without being illegal or physically dangerous. It flies under the addiction radar of the "this is how you make a *bad* decision" meter. It's seems harmless (and it also gives the appearance of resolving our aloneness). Many people urge their kids to get off the video games. Yet, in the morning, they themselves open their eyes to the sound of a vibrating text message on their cell phone and grab the unit because someone needs us. Maybe we, too, want to be relevant, not alone.

Disinterest in finding and hearing God is fed by television and social media, along with a variety of entertainment options. Television conditions us with the notion that it is normal for people to speak more than listen. Talent judging shows represent celebrities sitting on a panel or at a desk and critiquing others about their performance or speaking out on a particular topic to draw the listener into their way of understanding and reinforce mob-like reasoning. You will never hear the voice of the Holy Spirit use this tactic! We prop up their opinions, as if they meant something, agreeable or disagreeable, and then we choose a side. Taking sides makes us feel better about ourselves because we are, once again, not alone. Moreover, we have joined forces with the ruling voices of the television show—often those "in the know" or the "winners" of the talent prize. *We are on the right team,* we tell ourselves silently.

At this juncture, we have infected our decision-making process with a virus that is undetectable and has only one cure—God. So, like a drug addict, these social and entertainment addictions work on us at a much deeper and concealed level. They introduce fears, anger, and frustration, which break us down at the root of our being. They also expose us, and we experience the loss of self-control. If we don't have the ability to "talk ourselves down from the ledge," we wind up spiraling deeper into poorer and poorer decision-making, or perhaps no decision-making at all. This ignites the doubt that destroys lives—all related to the critical process of choosing elements that influence our decision-making process.

Deception by the Physical

The voice of God is the only meter for determining whether something is good or evil. Some would make an argument for conscience. I only disagree on this point because Paul says the conscience can become callous via scorching.

But the Spirit says explicitly that in later times some will fall away from the faith, paying attention to seducing spirits and teachings of demons. In the hypocrisy of those who speak lies, they are scorched in their own conscience. They forbid marriage *and command to abstain* from foods which God created to be received with thanksgiving by those who are faithful and know the truth. For all that God created is good, and nothing is to be rejected, if it is received with thanksgiving. (1Timothy 4:1–4 MW)

This callousness can be validated by exploring the topic of human sexuality. Sex is an excellent example of a physical action that leads to a false positive in terms of hearing the voice of the Holy Spirit. This powerfully natural force can invoke our emotions in a way that overpowers the relationship with God. Humanity's understanding of sex has primarily found its way to us from all directions—except vertically down from God. Yes, we have the Song of Solomon, but it pales in comparison to all the other widespread secular data available. Today, media does more than books did for centuries. The eyes can now see what the mind concocts. For example, popular films have portrayed sex as a horrendous event of physical abuse, especially for women and children. But they also portray sex as an amazingly beautiful, almost unattainable, experience. The consummation that should be reserved for a God-ordained union is portrayed as unnatural and disgusting because we have seen the abuse and violation of the human body by evil in the real world. But physical intimacy has also been portrayed to be beautiful and unreachable because it is only part of the human experience of trust and is short-lived because it disappears so quickly. In the film *Gladiator,* the character of Richard Harris, who plays Caesar, says the following, "There was a dream that was Rome. You could only whisper it. Anything more than a whisper and it would vanish, it was so fragile"[6]

There is a dream that is intimacy, as portrayed by Hollywood, but just the mention of the type outstanding intimacy experiences in real life simply vanish, just by a whisper. This sentiment is shared by many today in lieu of God's view found in the Bible. The beauty that God offers as a precious gift to the heart is swallowed up by the mind of decay because of a failure to discern the voice of God. The visual sexual experience on a movie screen is not an example of a God-ordained intimate relationship. It is a deceptive lure that causes viewers to think they can duplicate what they witnessed without God's connection. And once again, it is our aloneness that validates my words.

An intimate human relationship goes far beyond the physical. It is about trust. But the deceptive nature of physical union devoid of trust leads to many levels of hurt. The evil we see in relation to sexual activity causes the conscience to become calloused. We think we have the knowledge of good and evil. Yet, we cannot measure good and evil in relation to our flawed understanding. The greatest area of deceit is found in what appears "good" but is really evil. Adulterous liaisons are frequently portrayed in film as glorious, uplifting experiences minus the reality of broken hearts, broken vows, and broken families. Ironically, aloneness can be magnified many times over when we become involved with the wrong person in a self-deceptive relationship.

The voice of God, His Holy Spirit, is direct and truthful. The lesson is that the human good/evil meter is meaningless without God. Humans have existed from the beginning of time without the ability to understand their moral meter is broken. A new television talk show host pointed out that we can go back in time and historically recognize that we cannot recognize evil. It keeps revisiting humankind because humankind refuses to acknowledge the one true God, His Son the Messiah, and His Holy Spirit. The relationship with the latter provides the real meter for good and evil.

How Little We Know — Especially about Ourselves

Capably incapable is my description for humankind. We think we know so much about everything, but we really don't. Consider how human knowledge is diluted. As a healthcare professional, I have seen the medical profession transition dramatically. Years ago, the general practitioner discipline comprised the vast majority of medical doctors. Today, we have specialties in medicine that care for the smallest parts of the human body. Our knowledge is vast because of the vastness of creation. Yet, the more we know, the more we grasp how little we actually know, a marginally agreed-upon position.

Consider the following. God has allowed humankind to be deluded with knowledge. Humans have arrived at conclusions about which no true understanding exists. We continue to discover "new" information daily. In many cases, it contradicts previous conclusions. I remember the Woody Allen movie *Sleeper*. When the sleeper wakes up, people are consuming chocolate and sweets as a majority of their diet, and this conversation takes place:

Dr. Melik: This morning for breakfast he requested something called "wheat germ, organic honey and tiger's milk."

Dr. Aragon: [chuckling] Oh, yes. Those are the charmed substances that some years ago were thought to contain life-preserving properties.

Dr. Melik: You mean there was no deep fat? No steak or cream pies or . . . hot fudge?

19

Dr. Aragon: Those were thought to be unhealthy . . . precisely the opposite of what we now know to be true.

Dr. Melik: Incredible.[7]

Yes, this is comedy, but as a pharmacist I have seen study after study contradicted by subsequent research.

Now, God understands humanity, His creation, as indicated in this passage from Genesis:

> And the LORD said, "Behold, they are one people, and they all have the same language. And this is what they began to do, and now nothing which they purpose to do will be impossible for them. "Come, let Us go down and confuse their language, that they may not understand one another's speech." So the LORD scattered them abroad from there over the face of the whole earth; and they stopped building the city. (Gen 11:6–8 NASB)

God knows our potential, our audacity, and our propensity for evil, and yet He still loves us. The voice of the world teaches us that we will be respected and honored because of personal attributes or accomplishments. The voice of God tells us the opposite—that we will be loved simply because God created us to be with Him.

The general problem of the world's view is the source of information by which we are evaluated. When compared to God, what humankind actually has at its disposal is something akin to the "Magic 8" ball. You remember that toy in the design of a number 8 billiards ball. It was water-dyed dark blue and had a see-through window. You shook it up, and, magically, a message for you would appear in the window from the murkiness of the liquid.

The twenty answers inside a standard Magic 8-Ball are:

- It is certain. It is decidedly so. Without a doubt. Yes definitely. You may rely on it
- As I see it, yes. Most likely. Outlook good. Yes. Signs point to yes

- Reply hazy try again . Ask again later . Better not tell you now . Cannot predict now
- Concentrate and ask again . Don't count on it . My reply is no . My sources say no
- Outlook not so good . Very doubtful

Would you run your life by these twenty answers? I know, it sounds foolish because we know so much more than eight possible solutions to the challenges of our lives or the challenges to humankind at large. This is simply a comparison to how God makes decisions. "For *as* the heavens are higher than the earth, So are My ways higher than your ways, And My thoughts than your thoughts" (Isa 55:9 NASB).

I have found that the voice of the Holy Spirit speaks truth. Truth is different from facts. Truth is how facts are interpreted. Truth exists in God, and in God, The Son, Jesus. This truth has been delivered throughout time by God the Holy Spirit. Here is a simple, you might even consider it silly, story about truth. I was out jogging and praying one day. Out of nowhere the Holy Spirit said to me, "Did you know Jesus is like a Christmas tree?" Since it was July, I was somewhere between bewildered and intrigued. So, I replied, in a thought, "How is that?" He said, "When you decorate your Christmas tree, you put so many ornaments, extensive garland, and decorous lights on it that it obscures the tree that you really don't see it."

What the Holy Spirit was helping me realize is that the conventional church has put so much doctrine and organized information in its message of Jesus that He has become insignificant, irrelevant, and obscure. His message is diluted and convoluted because attendance, money, notoriety, marketing, and bling are what grab churchgoers' attention. The church is afraid that "Jesus" is not enough and that the Holy Spirit needs our help. The only reason why it appears this way is because people will not allow Him to speak. They refuse to spend time with Him because they don't want to listen for His voice or don't understand that they can. People "know" that this message is outdated, simple and narrow.

21

Earthly success is more important than their heavenly ascent. Jesus descended to a lower position before attaining the highest one. Our path must be similar. "If you want to win, you need to lose." Submitting to the voice of the Holy Spirit will reorient our thoughts, feeding our desire to hear further from God.

THE PROBLEM WITH DOCTRINE

The Bible versus Religion

A s a teacher and communicator, I have, over the years, had times when what my listeners heard was different than what I was saying — or trying to say. Where the Bible is concerned, this same dilemma has plagued readers and has been a source of contention over many centuries. Do we do what the Bible says, or do we do what we think it means to say, or what we want it to say?

This is a relevant issue not only for the Bible but also our nation. The constructs of the Constitution came from humans who had particular understanding in a particular window of time. Today, there are various interpretations of those laws that are argued in the courts. The meanings of words change with each generation.

So, we cannot attempt to understand the Bible without risk. Those who recognized the risks took what the Bible says or means to say and protected it by constructing some type of fence to protect it. This is called a doctrine. A doctrine is meant to prohibit varied possibilities where meaning and interpretation are concerned. Constructing doctrine, and ultimately forming theology, has reared the ugly head of formalized religion through the centuries because, as the word *religion* means to bind, denominational doctrines were meant to bind the members of these organizations to specific practices, procedures, and conclusions. This has caused humankind to do exactly what God opposes, directing the unit of the individual away from the unity of God. Religious doctrinal theology arrogantly claims that it understands completely about God, who He is, how He thinks, what He will do, what He wants us to do, where He is, and more. Religion believes it even understands the being of God. As my good friend Dan Gruber says, "Christianity claims to have all the answers when in fact they really don't even know the correct questions."

We must learn to discard doctrinal Bible bias so we can converse with the Holy Spirit in a manner that unbinds the individual. Conversing with the Holy Spirit, in part, means to ask questions and to receive direct feedback that gives you the opportunity for a rebuttal. Doctrine eliminates this process. It asks all the questions and receives all the answers. If you will agree with me that our knowledge is limited and remember that truth is not cognitive knowledge—it is an experience—you can then begin to understand that there is a process involved in the progress of each human being. Here is an example of a process whereby doctrine and growth collide head-on.

On a regular basis I hear people near and far say, "I hate my job; I want to do work I love."

My response each time is this: "Don't focus on doing what you love; learn to love what you do." If people want to change their job, that is fine, but until then I suggest they keep this principle in mind. The credo of society today is, "Be happy!" Sports figures do a job that is really not a job. It is really cool to "play" and get paid for it. It makes many people, like a pharmacist, say, "Hey, I have all this stress in my job. I would like to do something I really love, like play baseball." But just having a negative attitude testifies to our brokenness. Chuck Swindoll gave us a quote that I believe is as close to Scripture as a modern-day person can get. It is titled "Attitude":

> The longer I live, the more I realize the impact of attitude on life. Attitude, to me, is more important than facts. It is more important than the past, than education, than money, than circumstances, than failures, than successes, than what other people think or say or do. It is more important than appearance, giftedness or skill. It will make or break a company . . . a church . . . a home. The remarkable thing is we have a choice every day regarding the attitude we will embrace for that day. We cannot change our past . . . we cannot change the fact that people will act in a certain way.

We cannot change the inevitable. The only thing we can do is play on the one string we have, and that is our attitude . . . I am convinced that life is 10% what happens to me and 90% how I react to it. And so it is with you . . . we are in charge of our attitudes.[8]

Attitude control is not possible without the Holy Spirit. It is only a symptomatic reflex to a manipulative, broken mind. Unhappiness with one's job and the attitude that accompanies it is a matter of daily experience, but over time with increased stress, it cuts into us as a matter of urgency and "burn-out." When my sons were growing up, even now sometimes, chores are required. When they were young, they had to pick up their toys. As they grew, they helped with dishwashing, dusting, gardening, and more. They had friends who were able to bypass these uncomfortable chores and run the streets having a "good time." It was always a struggle to get our boys to enjoy these tasks.

Now this is where wisdom is concerned. On Sundays, my eldest son John and his family would visit. If I was working outside in the yard, he would come out to see if I needed help. All of his brothers were either in the military or away at school. Ultimately, each of them as they matured offered the same help when they saw a need. The doctrine of chores became the "responsibility" of chores. They began to lose sight of the task and exchange it for the "charge" of being a Diomede. They realized they represented something bigger than their own desires.

John the Baptist was born to a priestly line and was destined to serve in the Temple, a high honor. But he decided to forego that and listen to the Holy Spirit. Jesus knew exactly who He was, the King of Israel, but He hearkened to the voice of the Holy Spirit who charged Him with His servant duty:

Who has believed our message? And to whom has the arm of the LORD been revealed? For He grew up before Him like a tender shoot, And like a root out of parched ground; He has no *stately* form or majesty That we should look upon Him, Nor appearance that we should be attracted to Him.

He was despised and forsaken of men, A man of sorrows, and acquainted with grief; And like one from whom men hide their face, He was despised, and we did not esteem Him. Surely our griefs He Himself bore, And our sorrows He carried; Yet we ourselves esteemed Him stricken, Smitten of God, and afflicted. But He was pierced through for our transgressions, He was crushed for our iniquities; The chastening for our well-being *fell* upon Him, And by His scourging we are healed. All of us like sheep have gone astray, Each of us has turned to his own way; But the LORD has caused the iniquity of us all To fall on Him. He was oppressed and He was afflicted, Yet He did not open His mouth; Like a lamb that is led to slaughter, And like a sheep that is silent before its shearers, So He did not open His mouth. By oppression and judgment He was taken away; And as for His generation, who considered That He was cut off out of the land of the living, For the transgression of my people to whom the stroke *was due*. His grave was assigned with wicked men, Yet He was with a rich man in His death, Because He had done no violence, nor was there any deceit in His mouth. But the LORD was pleased to crush Him, putting *Him* to grief; If He would render Himself *as* a guilt offering, He will see *His* offspring, He will prolong *His* days, And the good pleasure of the LORD will prosper in His hand. As a result of the anguish of His soul, He will see *it* and be satisfied; By His knowledge the Righteous One, My Servant, will justify the many, As He will bear their iniquities. Therefore, I will allot Him a portion with the great, And He will divide the booty with the strong; because He poured out Himself to death, And was numbered with the transgressors; Yet He Himself bore the sin of many, And interceded for the transgressors. (Isaiah 53:1–12 NASB)

Most of us understand Isaiah 53 to be a Messianic scripture. When reading these words, we can all agree that we are very glad they were not meant for us. Who would want to go through this? I daresay that the Bible even records that Jesus looked for a different way to fulfill His mission. Yet, He did not despise His task:

> Therefore, since we are surrounded by so great a cloud of witnesses, let us also lay aside every weight, and the abundant sin around us. And let us run with patience the race that is set before us, looking to Jesus, the author and finisher of the faith He <u>endured the cross because of the joy set before Him</u>, despising the shame, and sat down at the right hand of the throne of God. (Hebrews 12:1–2 MW)

Jesus accepted what He had to do, even though it was unpleasant. He embraced His role as the Son of God and the Representative of humanity. He did not seek to be crowned King, even though He was the King:

> For let this mind be in you which was also in Messiah Jesus. Existing in the form of God, did not think of equality with God a prize to be grasped. He emptied Himself instead taking the form of a bond-servant, being made in the likeness of men. And being found in form, He humbled Himself, becoming obedient to death, yes the death of the cross. Therefore, God also highly exalted Him, and gave to Him the name which is above every name, (Philippians 2:5–9 MW)

Jesus did not seek divinity for personal aspirations. He learned to love what He did because He focused on the voice of the Holy Spirit. He did not equate religion and doctrine with relationship, belonging to no particular synagogue congregation. He allowed the charge of relationship and responsibility to override doctrinal limitations, something that my sons also learned in part, and become unbound to work for the Kingdom of God, not human organizations.

Doctrine is the result of both fear and a lack of faith. It can be very challenging and dangerous in religion. Christian doctrine controls various organizations, their movement, and the movements of their adherents. Members of the "church" are manipulated into a cyclical downward spiral as they consider what they read in the Bible under the umbrella of their own doctrinal rules, forming their theology. Each of us should hear from the Holy Spirit, but church leadership often prevents this:

> "Woe to you Torah Scholars and Perushim, pretenders! For you travel around by sea and land to make one proselyte; and when he becomes one, you make him twice as much a son of Gehinnom as yourselves!" (Mathew 23:15 MW)

Power corrupts! Leadership learns doctrine through an often-rigid educational conditioning system. And the claim becomes, "Now the Bible, a mystical book, is beyond the grasp of the "regular" person." The vast majority of people I have encountered over the years said they just could not understand the Bible. It is too complicated. On the other hand, atheists such as Sam Harris cannot believe the massive following of a book that contains such outdated and limited information.

Some teachers and preachers will go on for hours about what the Bible means to say. They are its interpreters for the masses. These individuals appear to be mystically connected to or hearing directly from God, just like the writers of the biblical books. To the hearer, these individuals "hear better," as these interpreters convey a sense of being closer to and knowing more about God than others. Two classes of people have evolved, thus fulfilling the ultimate goal of such organizations, which is power through knowledge (Genesis 3:5). Power corrupts—and teachers should heed James who says, "My brethren, do not become many teachers, knowing that we will face a more demanding judgement" (Jam 3:1 MW).

There are many approaches to deciphering biblical writings and discerning the voice of God. We should be teaching people to seek this goal and hear the voice of the Holy Spirit, not forming conclusions for them. The standard way of doctrinal formation employed by most organizations is to link various biblical sections together in order to support their beliefs. Indoctrinating the Bible has been at the root of religious schisms since their inception. Because the individuals of the Bible can be very difficult to know, we must try to set aside doctrine and attempt to engage in a fresh comprehension, even if our conclusion is that we don't understand! Ultimately, there is enough biblical direction about living in a godly manner for us to gain something positive from its content. This simple and humble approach is often ignored, even blocked by leadership.

The Doctrine of Who, What, When, Where, Why, and How

Much of this writing warns of the dangers of doctrine. While the bondage of listening to what organizations concluded about what God says is problematic, God has allowed it for our good. Most of us know what it feels like to be healthy. Without this information, we would never know the difference between health and sickness. This section is a composite of thoughts we need to evaluate about some biblical complexities, some human complexities, some creation complexities, and some God complexities. Please bear with the subject matter as I present the thoughts for your consideration. Thoughts that can help us to discern health from disease.

When I was young, my older brother Ed would call me "the computer." He said it was because I had an answer for everything. I think to some extent, he was correct about humanity. When humans are born they have little communicative working data and no words to represent themselves. All communication is sourced from the body. In this newborn, the body is master. The body's needs drive the behavior of the child. It cries when hungry or uncomfortable. It excretes waste on its own schedule. It rests or is active as the body determines. Parents throughout the ages would all love to have some say in the matter, but they don't. As we grow, so does our communicative data.

Communicative data, our words or mind, is like RAM memory in a computer. It functions relative to the accumulation of total data (the hard drive). The spirit is similar to the motherboard, hardwired for a specific function, to hear from The Holy Spirit. So spirit, soul (mind/words), and body all have individuality seemingly related to function. As the human grows, data begins to be stored in the mind. This working knowledge eventually interacts with the rest of the person in an interesting way. As the individual

29

accumulates data, or information, the mind finds or learns that it has some say in bodily matters and eventually exerts significant control over the body. The spirit needs the mind's control because in and of itself, it cannot control the body.

In the case of humans, over time what develops is a relationship among the three. This relationship is mostly defined by conflict, rarely agreeing on anything, characterized by our ability to complain. The spirit's function is primarily focused on determining right from wrong. We could refer to this as the conscience, but it is not that simple. The mind, for the most part, controls the representation of the spirit and the body, this is who we are to others. The body exerts some control at times, especially when I want that last piece of chocolate mousse cake, and so the battle is real. In the case of an actual computer, the components function together to a particular end. But they, the motherboard, RAM, and hard drive, are all individual pieces. This very crude example of life acting out, either as a human creation or in the image of God, allows the Creator to expand our thinking so as to consider the effect of the Holy Spirit, input from the keyboard, on our lives.

Hearing from the Holy Spirit can be challenging because you cannot experience Him through physical senses. We humans, for the most part, think visually and imaginatively. We read about God in the Bible. Doctrine upon doctrine attempts to help us understand Him better. Time and place are not significant when thinking about God. Why? Because this is the most confusing issue surrounding Him. God exists outside of time. God exists outside of place. Time, place, and events exist in God. While this writing originally began to deal with the interpretation that the return of Messiah will be in physical form, it has grown to examine much more about Messiah, the Father, and the Holy Spirit. This is necessary because by examining the unity of God, we can distinguish properly between spiritual and physical.

The trap that we will avoid from the outset is the issue of doctrine about God to examine more closely a relationship with God. So, when I say "God," you must avoid thinking about the presets you have been exposed to, such as the Trinity, which means something to you. For now, let us simply speak about God, the unity, in whose image we have been created. Unity does not really mean anything to you, religiously speaking, but it is significant relationally speaking. One attribute to address is His omnipresence, a biblical concept supported by many scriptures. Psalm 139 is a good example of the extent of His omnipresence:

> O Lord, Thou hast searched me and known *me*. Thou dost know when I sit down and when I rise up; Thou dost understand my thought from afar. Thou dost scrutinize my path and my lying down, And art intimately acquainted with all my ways. Even before there is a word on my tongue, Behold, O LORD, Thou dost know it all. Thou hast enclosed me behind and before, And laid Thy hand upon me. *Such* knowledge is too wonderful for me; it is *too* high, I cannot attain to it. Where can I go from Thy Spirit? Or where can I flee from Thy presence? If I ascend to heaven, Thou art there; If I make my bed in Sheol, behold, Thou art there. If I take the wings of the dawn, if I dwell in the remotest part of the sea, Even there Thy hand will lead me, And Thy right hand will lay hold of me. If I say, "Surely the darkness will overwhelm me, And the light around me will be night," Even the darkness is not dark to Thee, And the night is as bright as the day. Darkness and light are alike *to Thee*. For Thou didst form my inward parts; Thou didst weave me in my mother's womb. (Psalm 139:1–13 NASB)

Omnipresence is the ability to be in all temporal and spiritual places at one time, or the attribute that actually places God everywhere at all times, including knowing the inside an individual, Kingdom citizen or not. God knows our thoughts as referenced in Psalm 139. His presence penetrates everything seen and unseen. Why? Because we exist in time, and He does not. It is like the ocean. Fish exist in it and need it to live. The ocean itself simply exists. It does not need anything to be the ocean. Humans have developed technology, such as sonar, to determine the location of objects in the ocean. God is much more sophisticated than sonar. If the water was a living being, like God, it could know the location of everything within it because the presence of the water is every-where concerning what exists in it. So it is with God.

Omniscience is the attribute of knowing the "inside" of the created being, along with knowing everything else. There is a simple thought to dispense with this so I continue the example of the ocean. Humans, the occupants, are mostly made up of the same substance, water. If the water is not only outside but also inside than the Life (God) penetrates every part of the creation. So it is with the Holy Spirit.

Since we are not omnipresent beings, although Facebook, Twitter, and a host of other sites make a valiant attempt to assist humankind in the effort to be omnipresent, we must understand that any omnipresent being must be beyond comprehension. To pursue this idea, we must consider that God is unique. The Jewish sage Maimonides states, "I believe with perfect faith that G-d is One. There is no *Unity* that is in any way like His. He alone is our G-d. He was, He is, and He will be"[9]. I don't fully understand why he references God as a unity, other than the Hebrew word for *unity*, which is *echad*, but it does speak to his deeper vision of God. God is not simply like us humans. Let us leave the door wide open, for your "camping-out exercise," and move forward.

The Bible states that God is a Spirit, and it also states that God the Father has location—on His throne. The Bible further states that God has appearance. Consider Ezekiel's vision:

> Now above the expanse that was over their heads there was something resembling a throne, like lapis lazuli (stone) in appearance; and on that which resembled a throne, high up, *was* a figure with the appearance of a man. Then I noticed from the appearance of His loins and upward something like glowing metal that looked like fire all around within it, and from the appearance of His loins and downward I saw something like fire; and *there was* a radiance around Him. As the appearance of the rainbow in the clouds on a rainy day, so *was* the appearance of the surrounding radiance. Such *was* the appearance of the likeness of the glory of the LORD. (Ezekiel 1:26–28 NASB)

And that His Throne is mobile:

> Wherever the spirit would go, they would go, and the wheels
> would rise along with them, because the spirit of the living
> creatures was in the wheels. When the creatures moved,
> they also moved; when the creatures stood still, they also
> stood still; and when the creatures rose from the ground,
> the wheels rose along with them, because the spirit of the
> living creatures was in the wheels. (Ezeekiel 1:20–21 NIV)

Imagine a motion picture cartoon where the ocean was all that
existed and it had life. It was alive, and it gave life to all that was in
it. Imagine further that the water could swirl together to form what
looks like one of the occupants of this life, like some of the structural
formations within it and some other creatures not often seen by the
occupants. This is what Ezekiel experienced. Ezekiel's vision is a
unique design because it seemed to have the spirit of the beings in it
as it moved. So, God has a throne on which He sits, but the throne
is not confined to time or space. Presence is also an interesting concept. Because of our human state, we believe that presence is confined to "where we are." But with the Internet and websites such as
"Go to Meeting," we can actually be in two places at one time, or
our "presence" can be. Is it possible for God to do the same without
being reduced to some type of radio signal? If not, He would be no
more sophisticated than us. Genesis offers a glimpse into this unique-
ness early on:

> In the beginning God created the heavens and the earth. And
> the earth was formless and void, and darkness was over the
> surface of the deep; and the Spirit of God was moving over
> the surface of the waters. (Genesis 1:1–2 NASB)

God did the creating, and the Spirit was hovering over the
water. Earlier, we read that the spirits of the beings around the
throne were in the wheels of the Ezekiel structure. I will define
spirit as the immaterial part of a being. This seems to indicate that
the spirit of a being can be located separately from the visible/other

part of that being. We know that where humans are concerned, the body is dead without that immaterial part of us. So, in the case of humans, the body and spirit must be together. Is the body the life of us or is the immaterial part? We also could consider that if this immaterial part of us is alive apart from the body, it probably contains our life and the data that is us. If you are saying to yourself, "this is confusing," you are correct. These are the conversations that lead to doctrines. Don't worry, I am not proposing a doctrine; I am just trying to expand your thinking.

Watchman Nee, an Asian Christian, who lived about one hundred years ago, says the best way to describe us and God is the term "will." He contends we are, at our core, "will." If we are "will," it may be why we live on. Will may be our consciousness. It may be life. In any case, we have been granted life by a being who is life.

Now, God and His Spirit are uniquely different from us, and this is where omnipresence comes into view. If the spirit of the beings moving the throne were in the wheels, how much more can God's Spirit be doing all that God wants to accomplish for us without being confined to His form or His location? As exemplified in Genesis, God's Spirit has individuality, but because He is life, life is in God and His Spirit. At the same time God is not separate from His Spirit because God is Spirit, and the Spirit is not something other than God: [24] "God is spirit, and those who worship Him must worship in spirit and truth" (John 4:24 MW). Isaiah says, "The Spirit of the Lord God is upon me" (Isa 61:1 NASB). So there is a reality whereby God and His Spirit can exist individually yet be One at the same time. This is the reality of omnipresence.

The next question is this: Do God and His Spirit think individually? The answer is yes, but this is complicated to explain because He does not think separately; humans do. In our own beings, we are prompted to move individually and separately. Let's call it our heart, mind, and body. Now, did you ever feel torn about a situation? I began playing golf twenty-five years ago. When I was playing, my wife was at home with three small children. After nine holes, I would lose concentration because my mind was thinking about my wife and kids, but my body was on the golf course. We all have experienced many such conflicts in focus. There seems to be the ability to experience some type of disconnect within the human being. These disconnects demonstrate that we have individual directions existing within us. We may not know the why, where, or what about this state; we just know it exists, and we can work with ourselves to make some sense of our existence.

This is true with God. We can work with Him, His Holy Spirit, even though we don't know the whys, wherefores, and whatevers of His existence. In fact, we can develop a relationship with the Holy Spirit to assist us in being unified in thought, word, and deed, just as God is unified. But similar to ourselves, God, since He is a unity, the Father, the Holy Spirit, and the Word of God all think individually but not separately. Thinking non-separately is defined as wanting what one wants. Thinking non-separately is defined by a desire for the common good leading to the common goal with the best results for all. Since God is all righteousness, there is never disagreement within His individuality because all three do what is good all the time and the Father seems to be the Director until He gave the Son all this responsibility. Because the spirit of an individual is like the God-centered hardwired motherboard of the unit and it receives input from the one on the keyboard, God's ultimate desire is that the spirit guide body and mind into paths of righteousness over and above the choices and voices of our existence. In other words, listen within for His voice.

Presence of God

The presence of God via the Holy Spirit is the focal point for much controversy throughout history. Jesus said that the Holy Spirit would be in us, and that is how we would know Him.

"I will ask the Father, and He will give you another Advocate, so that He may be with you forever - the Spirit of truth, whom the world cannot receive, because it neither sees Him nor knows Him. You know Him because He lives with you, and will be in you." (John 14:16–17 MW)

"However, when He, the Spirit of truth has come *He will guide* you into all truth because He will not speak from Himself. He will speak whatever He hears. He will declare to you the things that are coming. (John 16:13 MW)

In general, most scoff at the notion that someone can hear from God directly. There is nothing farther from the truth. In fact, biblically speaking, God has always wanted to interact with humans. The issue at hand is "Who hears from Him, when, how, and why?" God's Holy Spirit does whatever He wishes, using the godly and the ungodly. In the Bible, the Holy Spirit spoke to Moses and many others, and He spoke to ungodly Balaam along with Job's friends. For example:

Then God came to Balaam and said, "Who are these men with you?" And Balaam said to God, "Balak the son of Zippor, king of Moab, has sent *word* to me," (Numbers 22:9–10 NASB)

And it came about after the LORD had spoken these words to Job, that the LORD said to Eliphaz the Temanite, "My wrath is kindled against you and against your two friends, because you have not spoken of Me what is right" (Job 42:7 NASB)

God has a plan, and He will bring that plan to its conclusion. So, you may ask, can I hear from God? Most people probably do on a regular basis; the problem is weakness in their "trust" muscle. God is good all the time, but it is good not based on our understanding, but good based on His.

Let's look at Job. God allowed Job to be tested. God can and does use contrary circumstances to communicate with us. People don't want to hear this, but God uses sickness and other circumstances that, in our view, are unacceptable to grab our attention. Communication from God is not meted out on a reward-and-punishment basis: "Oh, I was involved in a car accident, so God must be punishing me for something." Thinking in this fashion is simply juvenile. One probably just needed to drive slower; it is all about decision-making.

As for the "evil" individuals of whom you might ask, "Why do they get away with acting in such a way?" God may not be able to get their attention in this life. But when and if He gets your attention, you might want to take the time to develop that relationship, so you can recognize His voice and guidance. Becoming familiar with God's Word is one sure way to develop the process of hearing the Holy Spirit. When you hear Him, it is usually an intuitive intrusion into your thought via a subconscious suggestion, a hidden meaning, a random choice, a prophetic revelation, a line in a movie, and more.

The presence of God can move on you like a warm breeze. As mentioned earlier, when it comes, it will apply to you personally. If not, it is probably not God's voice. If its application goes beyond self, so be it, but be very cautious. People have promoted much confusion when speaking for God unprompted by Him. Personally, I view the area beyond myself to be potentially dangerous territory. But I urge you to desire His voice, however it comes. I encourage you to seek His presence. Ask, desire, and hope "and hope does not disappoint us because God's love has been poured out into our hearts through the Holy Spirit who was given to us" (Romans 5:5 MW).

LIFE AND TIME

Eternal Life

As mentioned earlier, truth is an experience. One evening as I was watching the news, I experienced a moment of truth. Carly Fiorina, a US presidential candidate in 2015, was speaking about her daughter, whom she had lost to a drug overdose. Ms. Fiorina said, "Life in not measured in time; it is measured in love." When she said that, I experienced the voice of the Holy Spirit. The entire quote was not truth, but the first half is a word from God.

Eternity, a very popular topic among humanity, has always been something that escapes us. We make movies about it. We write songs about it. We do our best to understand it, describe it, and, ultimately, attain it. But we always put it in a context of time. After all, that is the only reference we have. The realm of God is an existence devoid of time. There is a relevant Bible verse recorded in the Gospel of John. Jesus was praying with his disciples in a very private gathering: "This is eternal life, that they may know You, the only real God, and Jesus the Messiah, the one whom You have sent" (John 17:3 MW).

I put this verse on my parents' tombstone twenty plus years ago. It spoke to me then, but only in shadows and mist. I knew it was of paramount value, but I did not know why. The day Ms. Fiorina made her comment it became clearer. If Jesus had filled in the second half of Ms. Fiorina's statement, I believe He would have said, "It is measured in relationship," because that is what He said as recorded by John when speaking about eternity. The full comment from the Holy Spirit was, "life is not measured in time, it is measured in relationship." Eternal life is relationship.

I may attempt to speak about the time part of the statement, but for now, I would like to focus on the relationship part, and I hope that will yield the time part. Life, the gift we all have received from God, has a life cycle that we are familiar with. We are born, we live, and then we die. This is all viewed through the telescope of time. We evaluate life within the borders of time, whether within the scope of our own lifetime or the lifetime of some other quantitative reference, such as the Bible or history or culture, for example. But we always are under the burden of time. Jesus never thought or acted under this burden. Look at the following verses:

"Your father Abraham rejoiced to see My day, he saw *it* and was glad." The sectarian Jews therefore said to Him, "You are not yet fifty years old, and have You seen Abraham?" Jesus said to them, "I assure you, before Abraham came into being, I am." (John 8:56–58 MW)

Martha said to Him, "I know that he will rise again in the resurrection on the last day." Jesus said to her, "I am the resurrection and the life. He who believes in Me, though he dies, yet will he live. Whoever lives and believes in Me will surely not die. Do you believe this?" She said to Him, "Yes, Lord; I have come to believe that You are the Messiah, the Son of God, the one who comes into the world." (John 11:24–27 MW)

Jesus answered him, "I assure you that unless one is born anew, he cannot see the kingdom of God." Nicodemus said to Him, "How can a man be born when he is old? Can he enter a second time into his mother's womb and be born?" Jesus answered, "I assure you that unless one is born of water and the Spirit, he cannot enter into God's kingdom. "What is born of the flesh is flesh, and what is born of the Spirit is spirit. "Do not wonder that I said to you, 'You must be born anew.' "The Spirit blows where it wishes and you hear its sound but do not know where it comes from and where it is going. So is everyone who is born of the

Spirit." Nicodemus answered Him, "How can these things be?" Jesus answered him, "Are you the teacher of Israel, and do not know these things? "I assure you that we declare what we know and testify of what we have seen but you do not receive our testimony. "If I told you things concerning the earth and you don't believe, how will you believe if I tell thing concerning the heavens?" (John 3:3–12 MW)

Each of these verses speak of impossible events when considered in time. Jesus challenges Nicodemus with the aspect of being reborn. I know my friends will say He was speaking about a spiritual rebirth, which is okay, but we should not minimize the fact that Jesus cared about Nicodemus and was challenging Nicodemus' understanding of the Kingdom and his relationship with God. He was having relationship with the individual; we have the opportunity to receive the event as an example of our potential relationship with the Holy Spirit. Jesus told Martha that He was the resurrection and the life. How can an individual be the resurrection? The resurrection is an event (in time?). At least that is our understanding. Jesus said to the group that Abraham rejoiced to see His day, and he did. The curious issue here is that His hearers questioned Jesus' age. Jesus said "Abraham" saw Jesus's day. Abraham, being dead, demonstrates that Abraham had a relationship way back then with God, and in fact, that Abraham lives now. Jesus was always under the burden of relationship: The relationship between Himself and the Father, between Himself and us, and between us and the Father are all through the Holy Spirit. Observe:

Thomas said to Him, "Lord, we do not know where You are going, how can we know the way?" Jesus said to him, "I am the way, and the truth, and the life; *no one comes to the Father, except through M*e. "If you have known Me, you will know My Father also. From now on you know Him, and have seen Him." (John 14:5–7 MW)

Once again, this seems an impossibility. How could a person be a way or path? And not only a way—but the only way! Why is

Jesus the only way? Because time only exists inside God and under the burden of relationship. Relationship with God is life. We think breathing or heartbeats are life.

In the movie *The Matrix,* two characters are inside a computer program practicing their martial arts. The one is breathing heavily because he is tired. The other asks, "Do you think that is air you are breathing, in here?"[10] Their actual bodies are sitting in recliners on a hovercraft. Everything they were doing was simply happening in their minds. My point is that what you assume to be relevant or important is not. And what you assume to be irrelevant or unimportant really is vital.

> Therefore, since we are surrounded by so great a cloud of witnesses, let us also lay aside every weight, and the abundant sin around us. And let us run with patience the race that is set before us, looking to Jesus, the author and finisher of the faith He endured the cross because of the joy was set before Him, despising the shame, and sat down at the right hand of the throne of God. (Hebrews 12:1–2 MW)

Prophecy promised Jesus's resurrection to relationship with the Father. For a period of time that we understand as three days and nights, Jesus existed without relationship with the Father. (I want to say this was like an eternity because it lacked relationship, but I have no accurate concept of that which I speak.). Life is not measured in time. God, the ultimate being, is life, He is eternity. His eternalness is somehow connected to His Being (unity), which seems to be our example for relationship, and ultimately life itself (which is in God).

Do you think it is possible that relationship exists outside of time? Probably not, because death terminates our earthly relationships. But remember, at the loss of a loved one, people are always saying mushy stuff, like "Your father will never die because he will be alive within you." My relationship with my earthly father continues to exist in my memories because the relationship was real and had sensory values. In that memory, he still speaks. So, the lesson is not about my father's existence but about mine. My consciousness can transcend time. Jesus' did!

I am of the mind that when people die, they do not cease to exist. So, what part of them continues to exist? We know there is a body involved, data, and will, which consists of that part of us that manages the data. Since the dead, in my opinion, do not cease to exist, then what continues to exist is the data and the will. Their container is meaningless for this part of the conversation. They continue to exist by virtue of relationship with God. Time is meaningless to life.

Let us look at it another way. If I were to put you in an empty room, you would not cease to exist physically, but relationship would cease. Life devoid of relationship is not life. Life involves relationship, not physical being. And if you were alone in a room, as you are alone inside yourself, without God, you have no life. You need relationship to have life; you need God the Holy Spirit. The risen Lord Jesus is example of this principle. His new container is very different than ours. It bears no burden of time or the temporal reality of His earthly life. It bears the life of "relationship," which is eternity. The Father, the Son, and the Holy Spirit do not know the limits of time because time only exists within the limits of God's plan for His creation. That creation is the recipient of God's Holy Spirit so relationship (life) can occur.

> But when the fulness of the time came, God sent out His Son, born from a woman, born subject to the Law. He did this in order to redeem those who were subject to the Law, so that we might receive the rights as sons. And because you are sons, God has sent out the Spirit of His Son into your hearts, crying, "Abba! Father!" (Galatians 4:4–6 MW)

God simply uses time to His advantage:

> He made every nation of men from one blood, to live upon all the surface of the earth. He determined appointed seasons and the boundaries of their habitations so that they would seek God, if perhaps they might reach out for Him

and find Him, though He is not far from each one of us. For in Him we live and move and have our being – as some of your own poets have said: 'For we are also His offspring.' (Acts 17:26–28 MW)

He placed each one of us here according to a timely advantage, so those that find Him can be destined for His Kingdom. Find Him, and you can find life. "Is that air you are breathing?"

The Knowledge of Good and Evil

W hen Adam was in the Garden of Eden, it was God who helped him and Eve understand. In a story relayed earlier, my sons were not doing anything evil by human standards when they did not respond to my calling them. While they heard, they were just not listening, understanding, and caring about my directions.

Much the same thing happened to Adam and Eve. At the moment they ate the fruit, while they heard God's voice, they did not listen, understand, or care about His instructions. They cared more about their own voice or the voice of the serpent, which offered additional information (knowledge) about the Tree of Knowledge of Good and Evil. I don't know what God spoke about with those two. They spent time every day with each other. God must have taught them something. I mean, after all, He is God and He has "all knowledge." So, how did they come to understand "naked"? God asked, "Who told you . . .?" Assuming animals talked and assuming they could be possessed by a demonic entity, Adam and Eve must have spoken with them on a regular basis. After all, there was no one else in the garden. The issue of nakedness was probably not an issue for animals, seeing as they are always naked. Was the fruit magic? I think not, only because the fruit would have been the culprit, not the three involved in the event. No, it was poor decision-making. The problem was centered on whose voice the pair heard and heeded. If they listened to the serpent on the first issue, then it is highly likely the serpent gave them other information. Who were they to believe? Again, "Who *told* you that you were naked"? Prior to this event, knowledge came from God's perspective. The Tree of the Knowledge of Good and Evil, I believe, did not infuse data into Adam when he ate the fruit.

I have a five-year-old grandson. He is a thinker. As his database of knowledge grows, he is becoming quite the decision maker. He has been told that playing too roughly with his eighteen-month-old sister was a poor decision. Occasionally, when he is of the mind to make poor decisions, he learns something as a result. It is called a conclusion.

Now Adam was far more intelligent than a five-year-old, so he probably drew some conclusions. The Bible verse says, "They realized they were naked." How exactly does this happen? It is a lightbulb moment. One minute it was meaningless; the next it was meaningful. Knowledge from the serpent gave Adam the opportunity to draw a conclusion, that he, Adam, was capable of knowing something directly opposite from God's instruction. He thought he knew the difference between good and evil, but he simply knew bad decision-making. What this did was break the unity in his relationship with God. Additionally, to introduce separateness between Adam and Eve, it introduced curse. It introduced internal turmoil. As a pharmacist, I have for many years given out prescription medication to help people minimize or resolve that internal turmoil. Sometimes it is not an easy fix.

When the serpent taught the couple what naked was, realization of new data made the internal turmoil worse because the direction of God now was missing. Most husbands and wives see each other naked all the time and feel no shame. This couple did feel shame, so they covered up; it was not always this way: "And the man and his wife were both naked and were not ashamed" (Genesis 2:25 NASB).

Only after giving place to another voice of teaching did the breakdown begin to spiral out of control. Shame is a painful emotion caused by the consciousness of guilt, shortcoming, or impropriety. So, the couple did not feel bad about their bodies, which is why most people feel shame when naked. Instead, they felt a tumultuous emotion. Individuals who frequent nude beaches do not feel ashamed of their bodies. In fact, they reverse the tumultuous emotion and project emotion toward shamelessness. Adam and Eve did not have the full force of sin yet, so they could not reverse project yet. This was new; peace had receded. Prior to this, all was good and calm. Body, mind, and spirit were in agreement. Now there was disagreement. The conscience, which emanates from the spirit, told the mind that it had done something it should not have done. Disobedience occurred.

> But sin, finding the opportunity through the commandment, produced in me all kinds of coveting, for sin is dead without the law. I was alive apart from the law once, but when the commandment came, Sin came to life and I died. And the commandment, which is for life, was found to be death for me, because Sin finding an opportunity through the commandment, deceived me and put me to death through it. (Romans 7:8–11 MW)

Sin became alive, and Paul became dead, relationally! Sin is lawlessness. Paul states that he was once alive apart from the law. A newborn babe has no sin and does not commit sin. This is innocence. But, at some point, direction, or law, begins to be given by overseers. The opportunity here is for that child to decide whether to agree or not. Will the child, relationally, be a good decision-maker or a bad decision-maker. Innocence departs. Decision making must become vital. Sin is not just an action or thought; it is a spirit and a demonic one at that. Why is it that you and I have "bad" thoughts at times? Temptation comes from humankind and from demonic influence.

Sin is alive. Adam invited another counsel to enter his decision-making process. The mind and the spirit are both susceptible to demonic forces. We have a society, at large, dependent on prescription medication. This is an attempt to disable the internal turmoil. The oppression that affects the mind is one level of attack. The oppression that affects the spirit is a deeper level, ultimately shutting out the voice of conscience and the Holy Spirit.

But the Spirit says explicitly that in later times some will fall away from the faith, paying attention to seducing spirits and teaching of demons. In the hypocrisy of those who speak lies they are scorched in their conscience. (1Timothy 4:1–2 MW)

Adam and Eve began to determine law for themselves, accompanied by the voice of sin, and became lawless toward God due to the lack of hearing God's voice. Adam blamed God for his new-found brokenness: "And the man said, "The woman whom *you* gave *to be* with me, she gave me from the tree, and I ate" (Genesis 3:12 NASB).

The voice of the enemy interrupted their lives, which is a further example of the loss of hearing from God. Their bodies and minds began to think differently than their spirit, which still had its godly connection. Conflict took over. What ultimately happened to Adam, and besets the rest of us, is that this internal conflict becomes our state of being. To heal the conflict, we use alcohol, sex, prescription medication, illegal drugs, food consumption, sports, television, smoking, material possessions, hobbies, vocations, vacations, and more. We need to feed our internal beast because intuitively we know something is wrong.

Money, power, or control is not even enough. Inner conflict gnaws at us moment by moment. We are so familiar with it that it has overtaken our airwaves. Television programs are all about conflict and mental and emotional abuse. We have no meter with which to measure. Our defense of ourselves is the proof of this. While people can seem to find solace in some of the items mentioned above, it is only temporary. So what will give our unit unity? It will take relationship with God, the voice of the Holy Spirit, a new direction, self-assessment, and a willingness to see the problem and change ourselves. All of this comes by learning to distinguish the voice of God from others. The knowledge of God trumps the knowledge of good and evil.

Silence

Sometimes the world seems like a lonely, empty place despite the billions of people who live here. Recent studies show that although communication has proliferated with the advent of social media and other forms of technology, an increasing number of people feel isolated and disconnected from society. Communicating through Facebook often leads to a false persona and unrealistic interactions that leave users even more lonely and alienated. We don't like silence.

A famous song from Simon and Garfunkel about silence called "The Sound of Silence" was very popular in the 1960s. It speaks of the fact that people often hear but do not listen. The song embodies an accuracy about humankind. Inside our head is solely our own voice. No one can get inside unless we allow it, and even then, they are not inside; we are revealing content. No one can hear our thoughts unless communicated. People can know how one feels, but no one knows <u>what</u> we feel. In general, we don't like the silence of other voices, the aloneness. Given the proper atmosphere, even introverts will communicate. We want to be heard. We want to be relevant. We want to be respected, popular, and deemed knowledgeable.

To avoid silence, people leave the television or radio on constantly as companionship as they move about their home doing daily chores. They hum, they whistle, they sing, and they talk. Kids run around the house screaming. The most difficult time is at night. They lay in bed with thoughts streaming through their minds, unable to sleep and unable to cease being alone. The catch 22 in this situation is that the companionship of aloneness gives us the power to choose what we let into the old echo chamber. Once again, the evidence of the corruption of power. This is why we need so many cable channels: some for shopping, for music, for movies, for religion, and more. We don't want to hear divergent opinions and views that challenge us. We have cornered ourselves into a personal, politically correct culture.

This is where the voice of God becomes most significant. I don't like the outside noise. It interferes with my hearing God. I hear my own voice, mostly in conversation with the Holy Spirit, I enjoy the lack of outside interference. I will sit in my living room watching a sports event or movie without sound. It gives me a chance to prioritize God's voice and helps me to know the difference between His voice and mine (at this point I am fairly confident of my hearing of the voices of the world and demonic influence). Hearing His voice lets me know that I am not alone—really not alone. I have a companion who is with me all the time.

My eldest son John is a verbal communicator. He always was. He was the kind of child that would answer the question, "How was your day?" with a monologue that could take you through dinner and dessert. God is not this way. God is a listener. As John matured in God, he began to listen, and you knew it. When God listens, you are aware of His presence and attention to you. He is not a fireman putting out our moment-by-moment fires. After all, He is God. What can surprise Him? He already knows 6 p.m. tomorrow. God spoke to me, as earlier mentioned, twenty years later on a specific topic. It is why you remember key memories from years ago. God speaks to you in your own language. He wants to draw off your emotion, and He wants His voice to be heard experientially. Communication is more than words with God. You only know His voice by truth, and truth is an experience.

In my relationship with the Holy Spirit, I wait, even long, to hear His voice, His timing, and His message. My friend Bill Fritzky has always characterized me as "camping out" on God's word, waiting for it to reveal itself. Let me give you an example. My twin sons, Steven and David, played football at a substantially expensive Division Two college. They received some scholarship funds, but not enough to cover about $20,000 of tuition per year. I approached them in their second year and tried to convince them to go to a less expensive school where, in fact, they would get more playing time. As I was having this conversation, the Holy Spirit said to me, "Did I ask you to have this conversation with them? Did I direct you in this area financially?"

When God speaks in this manner, it is not really a question. It is more of a rebuke. He does not want an answer. He was directing me to take an inventory of my will—to consider that my direction may take my sons directly out of His path. This particular inter-action brought fear to me because I never want to thwart God's direction, and we can if we are careless. Our fear can get in the way of God's plan. So, my relationship with the Holy Spirit led to more camping out. That is why when my third son, Christopher, said he wanted to disarm IEDs for the navy, I took my conversation to God. Christopher ultimately became a navy corpsman. In place of taking apart bombs, he was fixing people, which was God's path, not mine!

Communicating through a Mediator

Who is your decision maker? Being confused about making decisions is part of the human condition. What do I want for lunch? While walking through the mall, I pass an advertisement for a scrumptious-looking cheeseburger. There is an urge. Is my body leading the decision-making process? My emotions, my mind? It is certainly not my spirit because I really need to lose ten pounds, and my food choices have not been so healthy lately. It is all you, for the most part, having this conversation. But let's throw in a couple more players. You know who I mean—the evil messenger (devil) on one shoulder, and the good messenger (God) on the other. You've seen the TV commercial. The good messenger is encour-aging you to take care of your body, be healthy, and be happy. The evil messenger, on the other hand, is tempting you to take a big juicy bite, and you can eat better tomorrow. This is real life, and if you look around in the United States, you will see many people waiting to eat better tomorrow.

Demonic forces do not want to help humankind. Companies whose goal is to make money do not want to help people, unless it makes them money. In many cases, we find it a challenge to help ourselves. But God wants to help. God gave us a spirit, which is the conduit between you and the Holy Spirit. We hear not by having a little messenger sitting on our shoulder, but through the connec-tion of spirit to Spirit. This communication, like a radio wave, has signal strength. We can increase the clarity of the transmission by increasing the signal strength. This means static needs to be reduced, and if possible, eliminated. We need to hear the voice of the Holy Spirit through our spirit connection. Ultimately, the goal is the spirit of the human becomes the decision maker as it receives data from the Holy Spirit, who is the best decision maker.

Now, it is evident that guidance or mediation is valuable. God created us to go through the "hamburger" process for a reason. God wants us to be the decision maker, but we are broken, and the static exists. There is a battle for the reality of decision-making. The serpent in the Garden of Eden demonstrates this battle. It wanted to control Adam and Eve's decision by directing them. Adam and Eve failed because they allowed a mediator, who wanted to hurt them, to direct their choice. That choice, the freedom of choice, is a God-given right. Mediation is simply an opportunity for us to make wise choices.

John the Baptist announced the presence of the Messiah, Jesus of Nazareth. John came from a priestly family. Comparing his vocation to that of today's world, he was destined to take up the family business. He would work in the Temple, where the presence of the Lord resided. But John went into the wilderness, led by voice of the Holy Spirit. He chose to allow his reality to be guided (or mediated) by the Holy Spirit. He could have gone to the Temple, but he put organization (Temple) in its proper place. He was not enamored by what men thought was right; he wanted to listen to the Spirit of God. This man of humility, after receiving guidance from God, chose to deny his position in society and accepted his position in the Kingdom of God, all because he heard the voice of the Holy Spirit. Christian history views John as a larger-than-life personality. He was anything but that. When Jesus said that John was the least in the Kingdom, he was not speaking of position but was referring to attitude, he was a man of humility. John trusted God, not men.

Today Jesus wants us not to strive to become larger-than-life citizens of the Kingdom. He directs us toward humility. The voice of the Holy Spirit will always direct us accordingly. What we do in the eyes of our respective organizations, our churches, is not important; it is how well we hear and follow God. Allow God to be your mediator daily. Listen for His voice.

Putting Distance between God and Self

My relationship with the Holy Spirit leads to a similar experience characterized by 1 Kings 17:20. Elijah felt responsibility for how his relationship with God affected those around him. Hearing from and walking with God is a somber event that all believers should take note of. Now, I am not comparing myself to Elijah. But similarities in the "listening" experience bear some reflection.

I would not, for a long time, watch the movie *Noah* with Russell Crowe because I heard it was "unbiblical." One day I happened upon it as I was doing electrical work in my family room. I watched the entire movie. Biblical accuracy where movies are concerned is a dead issue. Writers and producers must embellish and alter certain aspects to draw viewers in. I get it! Sometimes they have an agenda. This is prompted by either interpretation or the overt desire to produce a message that causes people to think the movie accurately represents biblical account. I get that too! I not only enjoyed the movie, mostly because my expectations were so low, but also the Holy Spirit spoke to me through it.

After the Flood, Noah's character is depicted as becoming withdrawn. Whatever reason the writers had in mind is not relevant. The biblical account says he became drunk. What I began to consider was the magnitude of the experience of hearing from God, the responsibility of that relationship, and the result or consequences. When God speaks to me, and please note again, I am not comparing myself to Elijah or Noah, but there is still a weight to it. The Hebrew word for *glory* comes from the root for *heavy*. Having this relationship means that His glory, His communication, will weigh you down at times.

These are the times when I want to put distance between God and me. God's direction, in many cases, results in His people looking to escape it—like Jonah, the Old Testament prophet who fled in another direction entirely. We figure that if we get far away, the weight will lift. Some may refer to this as conviction. This is another way to recognize the Holy Spirit relationship. Recognition is vital for the successful walk of a believer. Surgeons open up a patient and must recognize the compromised tissue. This does not happen by coincidence. In the case of the surgeon it takes training. Recognizing those things that validate the God relationship only come because God has allowed it and because you have desired it. He can train you to see, hear, and recognize. Deafness to hearing God is like blindness.

One of the most majestic sights I have ever seen is the Grand Canyon. Everyone I have spoken to about this sight has not failed to recognize its majesty. The presence of God—the voice of God—can be just as recognizable. Another example is a baby. We have technology that allows us to see inside a woman's body and recognize the Creator at work. Yet, we have people who can see the baby but refuse to recognize the child. This lack of recognition is an act of will and a result of choice.

Jonah's decision to flee was an act of will and choice. Jonah was willing to die rather than let Nineveh off the hook for its atrocities toward Israel. But God had a plan, and He chose Jonah to bear that weight. He wanted to build Jonah's character for the Kingdom. There is an attitude that relationship with the Holy Spirit reveals, one void of entitlement and rich with servanthood. The feeling of heaviness from God is revealed and, at the same time, the realization of absolute need of God. We must move toward God into the weightiness of the relationship, fighting the tendency to put distance between Him and us. As we do so, His voice becomes clearer and more distinct.

THE VOICE OF GOD

The Desire to Know God

D o you want people to desire to know you? The human being is a complicated creation in some ways. Yet, in other ways, we are basic. We are simply "want-ers" at the core. Almost everything we do is done out of want. Self is our focus. Take a moment to do a self-test—the vacation test. Consider the emphasis or desire you put on going on vacation or just relaxing. Many hours of planning and thousands of dollars may go into just the leisure part of our lives. It gives me pause to consider the time and effort individuals invest in their vacations.

I know, you feel you deserve it, which brings me to another idiosyncrasy of us humans. Did you ever hear a best man's or maid-of-honor's toast? It is more about the toast-giver than the bride or groom. The reason is we want to define ourselves. To compound the matter, we don't like when other people define us. It offends us. The times we let someone else define us is when we know that it will make us feel good. We are prisoners of ourselves, bound in the prison of wants and desires.

God does not think in this manner. Remember, we are created in His image, not the other way around. Dietrich Bonhoeffer put forth a profound truth on this topic:

> It is a question of the freedom of God, which finds its strongest evidence precisely in that God freely chose to be bound to historical human beings, and to be placed at the disposal of human beings. God is not free from human beings but free for them. Messiah is the Word of God's freedom.[11]

54

God desires to be an example to us. Therefore, He demonstrates freedom, so we can grasp it and understand the desire to be free. Free from what, you ask? Freedom from the bondage of decay, freedom from brokenness, freedom from want, freedom from self. What, on the other hand, can we desire that is productive? I propose you contemplate the desire to know God. It begins with our allowing someone else, someone we don't know, to define us— namely God. This, of course, is problematic for many reasons. The types of challenges that arise are many: How can I know what God thinks if I cannot be sure that it is actually God with whom I am having a conversation? If I ask a respected religious authority, how can I be sure they know accurately? I am sure you can come up with a few other objections when it comes to the concept of being defined by God.

So, let's take part in a mental exercise. How about we bypass God and allow our enemies to define us. We cannot use our friends because we already know what they will say. No, I need people who don't agree with me. Next, I must consider their feedback as valid. This is very important. And we must keep in mind that the exercise does not include my defining them. This is about you; better yet, this is *for* you. And it is about your want (or desire) to know yourself or at least for you to validate what you know about yourself. Most of the time we are too busy defining that which is outside of us to pay enough attention to really define that which is inside ourselves. The truth is that we don't want to know ourselves. We want to know what we like to think is us. If we did, we would probably be repulsed. Don't agree? Here is the litmus test. Would you allow anyone, or everyone, to know what you are thinking at any, or all, times? Just place a little television screen on your forehead and let everyone see your thoughts all the time! Scary, eh?

God has given us a view into Himself. It is a book called the Bible. It may not be all-inclusive of God's thoughts, but it contains enough for someone to make a judgment. We judge God all the time. Why does God allow people to starve all around the world? Why does God allow sickness? But Jesus defined the Father for us in this manner:

So Jesus responded to them, "I assure you that the Son can do nothing of himself, except what he sees the Father doing. For whatever things He does, the Son also does these as well. For the Father loves the Son, and shows him everything that He Himself does. He will show him greater works that these, so that you may give honor. (John 5:19–20 MW)

Think for a moment about Jesus' life and deeds. God is who He is, just as you are who you are! You might ask, "How about the Old Testament? God killed people. Is this who God is?" Well, what is interesting is that God has just allowed you to define Him, my point proven. The difference between humans and God is that God allows someone like me, and many others, to write about Him and speak about Him, and when the opinion is negative, He is not reactionary. Thank God. His patience and compassion are boundless, as high as the heavens are above the earth. Right now we can see 13.8 billion light years away in the universe; who knows how far we will be able to see next year, since some theories suggest a constantly expanding universe? From my perspective, God's patience and compassion limits are unknown. From my perspective, I desire to know God because I desired to know myself. As for me, the verdict is "broken"! As for God, the verdict is Jesus. The Bible says it well:

This is the verdict: the Light has come into the world, and men loved darkness rather than the light, because their deeds were evil. For everyone who is doing evil hates the light, and does not come into the light, so that his deed won't be exposed. But the one who does what is true comes to the light, so that it may be revealed that his deeds have been in God. (John 3:19–21 MW)

As mentioned, our desire to know God is directly related to our desire to know ourselves. The truth be told, there are many things about myself that I don't like. I can do better. But doing better is a result of my inner person—my spirit and soul. Jesus indicated that our thought life is paramount: " but I tell to you, that everyone who gazes at a woman to desire her has committed adultery with her already in his heart" (Mat 5:28 MW).

The mind is an interesting enigma. It must be trained, like an athlete, a surgeon, or soldier. It must be taught what is good and bad, right and wrong. What you think about right and wrong is not important for the moment; what is key is that one understands that the human mind does get trained for both evil and good, and it also gets trained to desire God. Unlike animals, human want can be overcome by our gift of reason. Reason is the guardrail that keeps us on a particular road. The church (or any denominational organization), for example, has reasoned many arguments to keep themselves on a particular denominational road. Bonhoeffer said this about it: "Christianity conceals within itself a germ hostile to the church."[12]

Because of desire, we reason ourselves into getting more of what we desire. We reason ourselves into doctrine. We must learn to desire God. I have a pastor friend who lost his residence, a parsonage, because a church organization, led by another pastor, wanted a church building more than wanting a pastor and his family to have a roof over their heads. We cannot control our wants unless we direct them to the desires of God. We cannot know the desires of God unless we desire to know God.

Organizations, governments, churches, religions, and other institutions can be, and many are, based on humanity's misunderstanding of this principle. We must accept definition of ourselves from an outside source, namely God. We must consider either our own depravity or let our enemy's message provide insight into ourselves. Humankind is a broken machine, and we need compassion, mercy, patience, joy, and forgiveness. We will learn to desire God as we allow God into our conversation. " For thus says the LORD to the house of Israel, "Seek Me that you may live" (Amos 5:4 NASB).

Truth and Trust

What is the connection between truth and the human experience? We have a strong desire to define ourselves as truthful and trustworthy. That is how we tend to see ourselves. Even criminals make an attempt at truth by having a code of trust. When I was younger, an acquaintance who was older than me was having some marital trouble. He said, "It is amazing; my wife will let me see her naked but will not let me see her bank account." Imagine if Adam and Eve had bank accounts.

The comment stuck with me all these years, and I never knew why. I have come to realize that it was one of those puzzles that needed an answer. In fact, that is why some comments and events indelibly stay with us. We know the comment contains a grain of universal truth (it speaks to our spirit), but we just don't know how or why. The comment stays with me concerning trust, which I will speak about a little later.

When Jesus was speaking with the Samaritan woman, he gave her information that is crucial to understanding our relationship with the Father. The piece of information was that God is Spirit, and He seeks those who desire to worship Him to submit to Him in spirit and truth. The question we must answer is this: how does one worship in spirit and truth? Unfortunately, the church at large seems to believe that worshiping in spirit means an emotion of ecstasy, raising hands while singing, and having an unearthly feeling. This is not worship in spirit; it is dogma in action. Feelings are not relevant to worshipping in spirit. Worshiping in spirit has to do with being in touch with the Holy Spirit and acting as a citizen of the Kingdom and acting like the King, acting as Jesus acted.

Some of my friends will say the Holy Spirit makes them feel happy—emotional and ecstatic. Then, during a dry season, they feel like the Holy Spirit has abandoned them. The interesting thing about the Bible is we don't see this ecstasy at work. The presence of God is weighty and imposing. The communication of the Holy Spirit is judicious and penetrating. I taught a sermon on trust. It was the story of Jesus walking down the road where a blind man was calling out, "Jesus, son of David!" The Scripture came from the book of Luke chapter 18:

And he cried out, "Jesus, Son of David, have mercy on me!"

And those who led the way rebuked him so that he would be quiet; but he cried out all the more, "Son of David, have mercy on me!" Then Jesus stood still and commanded him to be brought to him. When he had come near, he asked him, "What do you want me to do for you?" He said, "Lord, that I may see again." Jesus said to him, "Receive your sight again; your faith has healed you." Immediately he received back his sight, and followed him, glorifying God When all the people saw it, they praised God. (Luke 18:38–43 MW)

First, notice that those who "led the way" tried to inhibit him, not uncommon in religious organizational leadership. But Jesus called the man over and asked him, "What do you want me to do for you?" Jesus knew the response but God wants personal interaction. The man answered, "That I may see again." Then Jesus said to him, "Your faith (trust) has healed you." How did his trust heal him? In the movie *I Robot*, the hologram of the victim kept telling the main character, "My responses are limited; you must ask the right question." In the film *The Matrix*, one character says to the other, "It is the question that drives us." Furthermore, my friend Dan Gruber said to me, "The church has all the answers, but they don't even know what the questions are."

So, here is the question. Is it possible for people to believe in something so strongly that they can make it happen? Did the blind man receive his sight because he trusted so strongly that he would? Was this measurable on the trust/strength meter? People who have their sight may have difficulty understanding this man's level of trust. I do! But sight was not the real issue; Jesus, son of David, was! Often in life, trust eludes us because we, in many cases, can make things happen. We can fulfill our wants because we live in a world where they are reachable. People who live on one-room boats in Asia without clothes, food, and furniture have cell phones.

Jesus himself asks another question: "…When the Son of Adam comes, will He find faith (trust) on the earth" (Luke 18:8 MW)? Faith, belief, and trust are, for the purpose of this writing, all interchangeable. Faith has become a "religious" word and therefore is a distraction. Belief and trust help us to focus less on religion and what we think we know about those religious words, and more on what we don't know. We can focus on simple relationship. This is important because it has all to do with the real concept of "trust."

Jesus said that if we can believe to the extent of the size of a mustard seed, then we can move mountains. The misconception is that the "quantity or measure" of our belief is key. This is not correct. It has no bearing on the *power* of belief. Why? Because we are not the ones with the power that moves the mountain. The power resides somewhere else. What is crucial is the *focus* of our belief, and focus can be just like a mustard seed, one concentrated point of truth that expands to be blessing for all who need a place to exist, that expands to the restoration of lost sight, an impossibility without focus on the King. "It is indeed smaller that all seeds, but when it grows it is bigger that all the herbs, and becomes a bush, so that the birds of the air can come and lodge in its branches." (Mathew 13:32 MW).

Listen to the blind man: "Jesus, Son of David, have mercy on me." His focus was correct. Initially, he recognized Jesus's majesty! It was not until he had Jesus's attention that he *asked* for his sight. The power to heal came from the focus, the pin-point revelation of Messiah's kingship and authority.

Too often I have taught incorrect principles about the Bible; the focus is not on humans—what we know or think we know, how strong our faith is, whatever that may be. The focus is on God and His revelation to us. "Your faith has healed you" was the result of a mustard seed of faith focused on the "center of the universe," Jesus the Messiah. He is the reason for and the center of the universe. He is the power of creation and the wisdom of the ages. He is one with the Father, a relationship we cannot understand, even in our deepest realms. No doctrine does it justice.

The Jewish Sh'ma says, "Hear Israel, the Lord our God, the Lord is One." The Jewish word for one is *unity*. God is unity. He is not alone, and aloneness is not His plan for us! He has given us each other to help us understand the concept of relationship. He has given His Son in the form of a human to seal that relationship. Our freedom came in the form of His death, and victory came through His resurrection. Overcoming our aloneness was sealed with the delivery of the Holy Spirit. It is the best medicine for what ails us. My friend Dan Gruber, in his translation of the portion of the Bible he calls the Messianic writings (more commonly referred to as the New Testament), footnotes the following verse from John's gospel as *a staggering claim*: "[6] Jesus said to him, 'I am the way, and the truth, and the life; no one comes to the Father, but through Me'" (John 14:6 MW). This is truth! Will you trust Him?

Believing Who Jesus Is versus Believing in Jesus

It never ceases to amaze me that Jesus was aware and, at times, revealed, who He was: God incarnate. Many, including His family, thought He was crazy. And why not? Think of the abuse and derision people experience who say they heard a message from God. Jesus was fully aware of His mission, and moreover, He had the courage and loved us enough to reveal Himself.

A Bible event details the death of Jesus's friend Lazarus. Mary and Martha, Lazarus' sisters, had a revealing exchange with Jesus:

So when Jesus came, He found that he had already been in the tomb four days. Now Bethany was near Jerusalem, about two miles away. Many of the Judeans had joined the women around Martha and Mary to console them concerning *their* brother. Now when Marta heard that Jesus was coming, she went and met him, but Mary stayed in the house. Then Marta said to Jesus, Lord, if you had been here, my brother would not have died. Even now I know that whatever you ask of God, God will give you." Jesus said to her, "Your brother will rise again." Marta said to Him, "I know that he will rise again in the resurrection on the last day." Jesus said to her, "I am the resurrection and the life; he who believes in Me though he dies yet will he live. Whoever lives and believes in me will surely not die. Do you believe this? She said to Him, "Yes, Lord; I have come to believe that You are the Messiah, the Son of God, *the one* who comes into the world." (John 11:17–27 MW)

It appears that Jesus was trying to expand Martha's thinking in several ways. Remember, He was not under the burden of time. To Martha, the resurrection on the last day was a time event. To God, the resurrection on the last day is a relationship event. This event exists "in Jesus." When my sons were younger, we went outside and played roller hockey in front of my home. The event existed in us because we were involved in it. If we do not perform the event, the event does not take place.

Events like resurrection exist in Jesus and because of Him, because He participates in them. Without His participation, it does not exist. He spoke of this concept to the Pharisees and Sadducees when He spoke of the resurrection and eternal life in general. He quoted Scripture: "I am the God of Abraham, Isaac, and Jacob." Then He said, "He is the God of the living." Life is an event that exists because God exists, and therefore, we can participate in it; God is life. Lazarus' story goes on:

When Mary came to where Jesus was and saw him, she fell down at his feet saying to him, "Lord, if you had been here, my brother would not have died." So when Jesus saw her weeping and the Judeans who came with her weeping, he groaned in his spirit, and was troubled. He said, "where have you laid him?" They told him, "Lord, come and see". Jesus wept.

Because of that, the Judeans said, "See how he love him." Some of them said, "Couldn't this man, who opened the eyes of the one who was blind, have also kept this man from dying?" Therefore, groaning again within himself, Jesus came to the tomb. Now it was a cave, and a stone lay against it. Jesus said, "Take away the stone." Marta, the sister of the one who was dead, said to him, "Lord, by this time there is a stench, because he has been dead four days." Jesus said to her, "Didn't I tell you that if you believed you would see the glory of God?" So they took away the stone from the place where the dead man was lying. Jesus lifted up his eyes, and said, "Father, I thank You that You have heard me. I know that You always hear me, but I said this because of the crowd that stands around, so that they may believe that You sent me." When he had said this, Jesus cried out in a loud voice, "Lazarus, come out!" The one who was dead came out, bound hand and foot with wrappings, and his face was wrapped around with cloth. Jesus said to them, "release him and let him go." Therefore, many of the Judeans who had come to visit Mary, and had seen what Jesus did, believed in him. (John 11:32–45 MW)

No one really understood who He was; they simply believed he was another, if not *the* messenger from God. First, the writer records that the people said, "Could not this man . . ." While a man, Jesus is much more than that; He is divinity. Mary and Martha both say, "If you were here, my brother would not have died." They believed He would have healed Lazarus and prevented his death. Time and place do not exist outside of God. God is not under the burden of time. Jesus, while he laid down his divinity to accomplish his mission, still had access to the power because He knew who He was, God the Word. In the case of the blind man, the blind man acknowledged Jesus's majesty. In the case of Lazarus, Jesus acknowledged his own divinity: "I am the resurrection and the life." Unless He exists, no one participates in life, there is no resurrection, and there is no life. Unless He gives it, there is no life. He honored the Father by this bold revelation. And the Father honors Him!

The office of Messiah is a significant attraction to many. The world, including Hollywood at times, puts forth "truths" of the universe in total ignorance of the validity of those truths. The office exists. The Messiah is real. Many cultural elements contain some type of "messianic" building blocks because the need for and concept of Messiah has been placed within us. We want to believe someone is going to get us out of this mess of a world we live in. Films such as *Gladiator, Terminator,* or *The Matrix* bring to life messianic-type characters. They are going to end the war and bring peace to the world! Yet, consider these words:

"Do you think that I have come to give peace in the earth?"
I tell you no, but rather division. (Luke 12:51 MW)

These movie characters generally have no clue of their significance in the scheme of society. As stated many times in the Bible, Jesus knew exactly what He was called to do. In pop culture, saving the world is the culminating event that eliminates the enemy, the Agent Smiths, the Commodus's, the bad guys. To do this, the "hero" must rise to the occasion to save the world from evil. The writers of such movies don't understand biblical messages, and thus the world's concept of Messiah is skewed. "And if anyone listens to what I say and does not believe, I do not condemn him. For I did not come to condemn the world, but to save the world." (John 12:47 MW).

In these stories of messiahs, when they save the world, the world has not changed. In the film *Gladiator,* after the bad guy dies, the spectators in the arena who yelled, "Kill, kill" were still the same people. Evil seems to center on one individual. This is not so. It is within all humankind. It simply exists on different levels. Evil's manifestation ranges from apathetic to zealous. Saving the world is done one by one. The world Jesus spoke of is within the individual, each and every person.

Understanding two truths is necessary. We must discover where we are on the evil-meter, and we must believe who Jesus is! When the script writer of a movie develops a messiah, the "human factor" always presents the character in paradox format. The paradox is "pride and humility" at the same time. The definition of pride is a person's sense of self-esteem or self-importance, the "I" or self of a person. But let's define ego as self-awareness. The character, at first, does not have this self-awareness. So, the writer develops the character's self-awareness over time. The unassuming nature or cluelessness of the character is apparent from the onset of the story. Epiphany or revelation makes the character and his or her destiny manifest.

We all relate to these messiahs. We want to be important like them, but we want someone else to say it. This trait exists in all of humanity, some to a less noticeable extent and progressing variably in all humans until we get to those whose self-awareness cannot be contained within the flesh. Jesus acknowledged who He was to

Mary, to Martha, to His disciples, and to the woman at the well, among others.

> The woman said to Him, "I know that Messiah is comes (He who is called Christos). " When he has come He will declare all things to us." Jesus said to her, "I am *He, the one speaking with you*." (John 4:25–26 MW)

Jesus is not like the messianic characters in film. The messianic problem is humans are drawn to the imaginary concept but reject it in reality. It looks good on the screen, but human ideology trumps God's plan. The world spirals downward because of bad human decisions. God reaches out to each person with His Holy Spirit in order to give them a new life spiritually. " Jesus replied, 'Very truly I tell you, no one can see the kingdom of God unless they are born anew'" (John 3:3 NIV).

God is not like humanity, which was created in the image of God. Because of our fallen state, pride and ideology have developed into a view that sees self and all humans in relation to what we think we know; hence, the experience of Adam in Eden. We must not be deceived by our vast store of information. True analysis of factual information translates into knowledge, which does not exist outside of Jesus. Great thinkers like Copernicus challenged the established knowledge of the day. The Messiah of the Bible challenges so-called human knowledge of all time.

> "You search the Scriptures, because you understand that you have eternal life in them. And yet these are they which testify about Me, but you will not come to Me that you may have life." (John 5:39–40 MW)

Today, those termed great thinkers derive their thoughts from the database of human-acquired information. All conclusions are based on that information. Information trumps relationship. Yet, from God's standpoint, relationship is everything—it is eternal life. The average person does not consider the vastness of what we don't know, just the mass of what we believe we know. Google will become the Gog and Magog information base of the Bible.

Let's consider the example of the age of the earth. I don't know how old the earth is, but any "conclusion" I make on that topic comes from data available, for example, either the information in the Bible or carbon dating and the earth's layers of crust. It is not enough to say "we don't know." This is the deceit that Adam and Eve bought into, believing they could acquire god-like knowledge by their own efforts: "For God knows that in the day you eat from it your eyes will be opened, and you will be like God, knowing good and evil" (Gen 3:5 NASB).

This is the pride of fallen humanity, the belief that we "know," and the surety of it. The amount of information we have ranges from nothing to very little about God's creation, and anything valuable can only be found in a relationship with His Son, Jesus the Messiah.

God understands our struggle: "Now when he saw the crowds he was moved with compassion for them, because they were troubled and abandoned, like sheep without a shepherd" (Mathew 9:36 MW).

He has complete understanding because He is God and knows everything. He has given us His written Word, prophets, and numerous representatives culminating with His Son, Jesus of Nazareth. Atheists, such as Sam Harris, cannot understand how one can make conclusions based on a script thousands of years old and written in times devoid of pertinent information. Jesus is not like the messiahs of Hollywood. He understood His value to the universe. He accepted His mission to save humankind. And He communicated to us through disciples who recorded His messages and the messages of the Holy Spirit. He continues to communicate to us today through the Holy Spirit.

We, like those messiahs, need time to realize the greatness and importance of the actual Messiah, Jesus. We must read His messages, such as, "I am the way and the truth and the life." We must realize that God does not view His self-importance as guesswork from what He does not know, but from what He does know. Our existence depends on Him because He is "The Life":

The Word of life is what was from the beginning. We have heard it, and we have seen it with our eyes. We examined it and our hands touched it. The life was revealed, and we have seen and testify and declare to you the life, the eternal life, which was with the Father , and was revealed to us. We declare to you what we have seen and heard, so that you also may have fellowship with us. Yes, and our fellowship is with the Father and with His Son, Jesus the Messiah. (1 John 1:1–3 MW)

The blind man's focus was on "the life." John the Baptist said that he was not worthy to untie Jesus's sandal. Peter asked Jesus to depart because he did not see himself as worthy of following Him. Paul called himself the "chief" of sinners and asked "who can save me from my own wretchedness?" And then he answered: "What a wretched man I am! Who will deliver me out of the body of this death? I thank God through Jesus the Messiah our Lord". (Romans 7:24–25 MW)

God, through His Holy Spirit, developed in each of these men a perspective that is paramount to the Kingdom of God: *who Jesus is*. If you develop that same relationship with the Holy Spirit, you will expand your understanding of who Jesus is. You will not simply acknowledge that He exists, and that will open the door to a meaningful and eternal relationship with Him.

Perspective

The Bible is a book that can be interpreted to say anything. This is due to individual perspective. Perspective is centered on having an attitude toward something. Perspective changes when the attitude changes. One of the greatest challenges to me is the perspective of the clear majority of Christians toward Christianity as an organization. They do not realize it embraces a mob-like mentality. In other words, many belong because others belong: family, friends, cultural adherents, and so on. Some people explain that they could never leave their denomination, church, or religion because of deceased relatives who were members at one time. Others are simply in bondage to a doctrine or a creed.

I was born into Roman Catholicism and was born again into Pentecostalism. From there, I moved on to Messianic Judaism, and I currently belong to a very small independent organization, only because the state requires an organization for someone to be a licensed minister. I talk with Christians, Jews, atheists, Muslims, Jehovah's Witnesses, and more. To put it directly, I am not into earthly organizations. There is only one that matters. It is the Kingdom of God as instituted by Jesus. Here is how He instituted it. Please read the content carefully (I quoted this scripture earlier but it needs repeating here):

> Who has believed our message? And to whom has the arm of the LORD been revealed? For He grew up before Him like a tender shoot, And like a root out of parched ground; He has no *stately* form or majesty That we should look upon Him, Nor appearance that we should be attracted to Him.
>
> He was despised and forsaken of men, A man of sorrows, and acquainted with grief; And like one from whom men hide their face, He was despised, and we did not esteem Him. Surely our griefs He Himself bore, And our sorrows He carried; Yet we ourselves esteemed Him stricken, Smitten of God, and afflicted. But He was pierced through for our transgressions, He was crushed for our iniquities; The chastening for our well-being *fell* upon Him, And by His scourging we are healed. All of us like sheep have gone astray, Each of us has turned to his own way; But the LORD has caused the iniquity of us all To fall on Him. He was oppressed and He was afflicted, Yet He did not open His mouth; Like a lamb that is led to slaughter, And like a sheep that is silent before its shearers, So He did not open His mouth. By oppression and judgment He was taken away; And as for His generation, who considered That He was cut off out of the land of the living, For the transgression of my people to whom the stroke *was due?* His grave was assigned with wicked men,

Yet He was with a rich man in His death, Because He had done no violence, Nor was there any deceit in His mouth. But the LORD was pleased To crush Him, putting *Him* to grief; If He would render Himself *as* a guilt offering, He will see *His* offspring, He will prolong *His* days, And the good pleasure of the LORD will prosper in His hand. As a result of the anguish of His soul, He will see *it* and be satisfied; By His knowledge the Righteous One, My Servant, will justify the many, As He will bear their iniquities. Therefore, I will allot Him a portion with the great, And He will divide the booty with the strong; Because He poured out Himself to death, And was numbered with the transgressors; Yet He Himself bore the sin of many, And interceded for the transgressors. (Isa 53:1–12 NASB)

God's organization is founded on this unique event that established a relationship between the Messiah and His followers. Day by day, His followers commit to doing His will. The Bible translations refer to it as "the church," but church has become a religious word that has created organizations with doctrines that usurp the original foundation, the boulder of His Messiahship as confessed by Peter.

And Simon Peter answered and said, "You art the Messiah, the Son of the living God." Jesus answered responded to him, "There is good for you, Simon son of Jonah, because flesh and blood has not revealed *this* to you, but My Father who is in heaven." And I also tell you that you are Peter. And on this bedrock I will build my community, and the powers of Sheol will not prevail against it."(Mat 16:16–18 MW)

The original word for *church* in the Greek was *ecclesia*. It means *assembly*. The word *synagogue* means "a gathering." There was nothing religious about these words to the biblical writers. In Jesus's day, the "church" was Judaism, large and small congregations formed by the lobbying of God's Word. Perspective is dynamic. Did you ever see those trick perspective pictures where the dark area is one image and the light is another? Different people, based on perspective, see different images, and at just the right moment, each person sees the other image. This I call perspective maturity, which can take time. Let me share a funny story.

In the 1970s, when I was about twelve years old, Newark Airport in New Jersey opened a new terminal. The highway logo was established for directing travelers to its location. When I first saw the logo, it appeared to be an egg-shaped, four-colored, shamrock-like visual. One early morning, some forty years later, I was on the way to the airport to pick up my Marine son who was coming home for leave. The year was approximately 2012. I looked at the airport logo and realized that the divider of the four colors was the shape of a plane. It's a plane I thought to myself! The logo was a plane! I had been to the airport hundreds of times over the forty some odd years and passed the logo many more times. For forty years, I saw what my perspective concluded as twelve years old. To see the "obscured" image, a mature and discerning change of perspective was needed. For all those years it was not important to me to discern the logo because I "knew" what it represented. I stopped asking the question. To mature in relational perspective with the Holy Spirit, we must begin with a question: who determines what is right? Jesus had the boldness to announce who He was:

> Jesus said to him, "You have said it. Yet I tell you that after this you will see the Son of Adam sitting at the right hand of the Power and coming on the clouds of the heavens." Then the high priest tore his clothing, saying, "He has spoken blasphemy!" (Mathew 26:64–65 MW)

> "For the bread of God is that which comes down out of heaven, and gives life to the world." So they said to Him, "Lord, give us this bread always." Jesus said to them, "I am the bread of life; the one who comes to Me will not be hungry, and the one who believes in me will surely not be thirsty." (John 6:33–35 MW)

Jesus had the Holy Spirit without measure. He heard and had relationship directly with God the Father. Following His ascension, He sent the Holy Spirit, so His people could, as a normal daily function, hear also. Hearing the Holy Spirit is of such supreme significance that Jesus's glorification culminated with His dispatching the Holy Spirit for all His people. For me, it is the entire focus for this writing.

God determines what is right, and He has made provision for His people to hear directly from Him, so He can mature their perspective. This fact has produced two results throughout history. One is that leadership is fearful that people will not hear them, so they block the freedom of believers to hear for themselves. They hold on with such a tight grip that the message of God becomes secondary, that message being that God wants direct relationship. The second result is organizations that so adulterate the Word of God they are labeled "cults." Within these organizations, the grip is even tighter. So, the universal symptom is doctrinal "grip." Within the Kingdom of God the universal symptom is Holy Spirit freedom:

> "The One who sent me is with me. The Father has not left me alone for I always do the things that are pleasing to Him." As He spoke these things, many believed in Him. Jesus then said to those sectarian Jews who had believed Him, "If you remain in My word, *then* you are truly my disciples. You will know the truth, and the truth will make you free." (Joh 8:29–32 MW)

I am not attempting to disassemble every assembly (organization). The focus is for the individual to deal with himself or herself concerning relationship with the Holy Spirit. How you respond to your particular organization is between you and God. God's focus on His Kingdom is a path that runs straight through each of us. And He made that path challenging:

> For the creation was subjected to futility, not of its own will, but because of the One who subjected it, in hope that the creation itself also will be delivered from the bondage of

71

decay into the liberty of the glory of the children of God. (Romans 8:20–21 MW)

He wants us to break out of decay into freedom. This is not an easy path. We can have a pity party. We can blame God for our lot in life, but that would be like blaming the person who pushed us out from in front of a moving bus for the limp we now have. When you miss the mark, it's okay; you are alone. You can admit this to yourself because God wants you to have two realizations. First, because you are alone, He is the only one who can help. The second is you don't need to be alone because the Holy Spirit wants to live with you.

When you walk with the Holy Spirit, judgment becomes a swinging hinge. I have many pastoral friends in churches that are guilty of bondage. These are not bad people; they are just cheated. When you draw your income from a certain source, there is an inherent fear of losing that income. This is not a church issue; it is a life issue. It touches everyone who has financial and social responsibilities. It is why humanity cheats at everything. So, being angry or hurtful toward church leadership is doubling down on being cheated. It may not be your job to call out the leadership.

The good that we think we can do is only good for some people. Sometimes, it is not good for anyone but ourselves. The ones who hear from the Holy Spirit should pray, support, and evaluate their role in that organization and the reality of their God-given freedom. There is existing leadership and organizations that you need to run from—I say run. Run fast and run straight to the Holy Spirit. Because we have not been taught the boldness to have relationship with the Holy Spirit on our own, our perspective is not maturing. Religion as an organization has been one of the greatest distractions for God's people. Jesus is the center of the universe, and He dispenses the Holy Spirit as He sees fit. For leadership, I say this: free your people. If they belong in your congregation, they will stay, not because they love you but because they love Jesus. Don't be like the leadership of Jesus's day:

"Woe to you Torah scholars and Perushim, pretenders! For you shut up Heavens kingdom in front of the people! But you do not enter in, and you do not permit those who are entering to enter." (Mat 23:13 MW)

Now just because Jesus addressed the scribes and Pharisees, His comment was not limited to the Jewish religion. Today, He calls out Christians and non-Christians with these words. Whether you are a church leader, a politician, a business owner, a worker, or anyone, He can speak to you through His Holy Spirit. That's why everyone must navigate a path toward God. That is a freedom that organizations cannot offer.

Of course, you will be mocked if you say you have "heard from God." Do not fear. Relationship is revelation. If you are spending more time with your organization than with the Holy Spirit, you need to change that. With the help of the Holy Spirit, you can differentiate the voice of self, the voice of the world, or the voice of the demonic from the voice of the Holy Spirit. He is all the discernment you need for a maturing perspective.

Hearing, Doing, Entitlement, Attitude, Compassion

On our mantel at home is a plaque that says, "Be kind, for everyone you meet is fighting a hard battle." For me, compassion is paramount. This does not necessarily agree with Paul in 1 Corinthians where Paul speaks of love:

If I speak with the tongues of men and of angels, but do not have love, I have become an echoing gong or a clanging cymbal. And if I have *prophecy*, and know all mysteries and all knowledge; and if I have all faith, so as to remove mountains, but do not have love, I am nothing. If I give all my goods to feed others, and if I deliver my body to be burned, but do not have love, it profits me nothing. Love is patient, love is kind. Love does not envy. Love does not brag, does not become prideful, does not behave itself inappropriately, does not seek its own, in not provoked, takes no account of evil. Love does not rejoice at wrong doing. But rejoices with the truth. Love coves all, believes all, hopes all, endures all. Love never fails; but where there are prophecies, they will come to an end. Where there are various tongues, they will cease. Where there is knowledge its use will come to an end. For we know in part, and we prophesy in part, but when the complete has come, the partial will no longer be useful. When I was a child, I spoke as a child, thought as a child, reasoned as a child. Now that I have become a man the things of a child are no longer useful. For now, we see an obscure image in a mirror, but then we will see face to face. Now I know in part, but then I will know fully just as I also have been fully known. And now these three things remain: faith, hope, love, but the greatest of these is love. (1 Co 13:1–13 MW)

Paul ends with the fact that love is greatest. While I cannot contest what the Bible says, in terms of message, I would like to contest the message the reader hears. The Greek word for love, *agape*, can also mean *goodwill*. The word *love* in our society does not necessarily encompass that semantically. The statement "I love you" is the most overstated and misused term in our society. For example, over centuries men and women became joined in marriage. The man vowed to love and honor his wife. Unfortunately, culture and society allowed, if not prompted, him to dishonor those vows.

The word *goodwill* brings out more respect than love. So for me, compassion is the goal, even though I fail at it sometimes. Semantic license for the word *compassion* is very narrow. If you walk by a homeless person asking for money, and you decline to act, you could claim love. After all, the derelict will only use it for drugs. But you cannot claim compassion because compassion speaks to being concerned for the sufferings and misfortunes of another. Compassion forces me to express concern. There are books on tough love. I am not sure about tough compassion. Compassion yields kindness every time.

Jesus went out, and He saw a large crowd. He had compassion on them and he healed their sick. (Mathew 14:14 MW)

"Now go and learn what *this* means, 'I desire compassion, and not sacrifice,' for I did not come to call the righteous, but sinners." (Mathew 9:13 MW)

"Being moved with compassion the lord of that servant released him and forgave him the debt. (Mathew 18:27 MW)

Now when he saw the crowds, he was moved with compassion for them, because they were troubled and abandoned, like sheep without a shepherd. (Mathew 9:36 MW)

So, how do we embrace this in a productive way? When we know the voice of the Holy Spirit, we can clearly hear how we should respond to various events in our life. John the disciple said one of the three types of sin is called "the pride of life." This part of our brokenness rears its ugly head in the form of the attitude of entitlement, which tempts us, and was addressed by Jesus Himself. This aspect of our existence causes us to aim our expectations in the wrong directions for insignificant or significant reasons. Jesus taught a parable about entitlement:

"But who is there among you having a servant plowing or keeping sheep, that would say this when he comes in from the field? 'Come immediately and sit down at the table.' Would he not tell him this instead? – "Prepare my supper, clothe yourself properly, and serve me while I eat and drink. Afterward you are to eat and drink." Does he thank that servant because he did the thing that were commanded? I don't think so. Even so, you also, when you have done all the things that are commanded you, say, We are unworthy servants. We have done wat we were required to do." Luke 17:7–10 MW)

The attitude absent of entitlement is diametrically opposed to human thinking. The attitude of "what is required" is a godly one. We view entitlement based on goals for this world, not on God's Kingdom. Jesus never acted entitled. He is the King of Kings but lived as a servant. The individual who hears from the Holy Spirit should be doing some serious serving, and that without complaining.

When I was married thirty-five years ago, husbands were the principal breadwinners. Women were beginning to join the workforce. Their primary job was raising the children and caring for the home. The culture we grew up in stipulated this pattern. It yielded some less-than-Kingdom results. My wife was college-educated and worked early on but chose to stay home and make raising our five sons her full-time job. She cleaned the house, did laundry, shopped for food, retrieved dry cleaning, prepared meals, and performed a multitude of other functions for our family. I held a professional job and did the "man's" chores, such as mowing the lawn, painting, and more.

As our sons grew up and went off to school, my wife began to work outside the home again. Sadly, over those years I developed a sense of entitlement. For example, I wondered why I ran out of clean clothes. As I became more in touch with the Holy Spirit, He beckoned me to begin doing some of the tasks previously handled by my wife. He said, "If you need clean clothing, then do the laundry—change your attitude." So, I began to take on some of the jobs my wife had been doing. After a while I began to get frustrated. This emanated from my sense of entitlement. But God pointed me to the above scripture. He explained that this, the laundry and more, was "required" of me—not by my wife, but by Him.

When I go to my pharmacy to work every day, the Holy Spirit "requires" me to care for people, to be compassionate. He requires me to be a good example to my sons, daughters-in-law, and grandchildren. God requires me to love my neighbor as myself. God requires compassion. God requires humility. Additionally, the Holy Spirit has informed me that someday God will require me to stand before the King and account for each of these aspects of my life. I cannot afford to feel entitled.

The Voice of God for His people

Elijah teaches us that the personal voice of God is a like a small whisper. God is not interested in commanding power; He has it all. He knows it very well because He is power. From a human stand-point, God is not interested in love. While God is love, our defini-tion of love is so distorted and tainted that we can hardly put our finger on the concept. The phrase *I love you* is a manipulative and misconceived statement in the human languages.

God is interested in intimacy. The Hebrew word for *intimate,* translated most times as the word *council,* gives an understanding of two people reclining and speaking to one another in close, thoughtful interaction. If you read the Gospel of John, chapters 13 through 17, you will see a true example of the intimacy of the voice of God. Jesus speaks of His intimacy with God while reclining with his disciples. We see a close, private, and intimate relationship. Over and over again, we hear the Son communicate the intimacy He has with His Father. Over and over again, we hear how intimacy translates into the love that exists between the Son and the Father.

The entire Bible speaks about this truth of intimacy. I want to speak about hearing God from a personal point of view because His Holy Spirit has taught me personally. The Bible demonstrates that God spoke to people throughout time. The enemies of God have attempted to distort His communication, love, and intimate rela-tionship by denying or misinterpreting it. It is up to us to learn His language, which is our own individual communication with Him.

I often reflect how I hear, think, formulate, communicate, and process all the thoughts that go through my mind. I studied Greek in Bible school, heard my relatives speak Italian, and encountered people who taught me words and sayings in Spanish, Hebrew, French, and other languages. My mind considers words in var-ious languages. My mind considers word pictures and images. My mind considers memories of events both from my life and from other people's lives. My mind considers what I read, what I see, what I hear, and what I do. This vast amount of information within us is at our disposal to hear and understand God's voice if we choose. More importantly, it is at God's disposal to use as He communicates with us. God speaks using all the aforementioned information of my life; God speaks to me in *John-ish*.

The two ways we hear are audibly and inaudibly. Audible language is well understood; inaudible is a little more challenging. I know you are thinking, "How can we hear the inaudible?" Hearing is simply a way of receiving data by our person. So is reading. We receive data from each of our senses. This data is processed in some way to achieve an ultimate goal, whether tangible, like a college degree, or intangible, such as experience. A review of the sources of data that come to us for processing in our lives is as follows.

We can hear the sound of our own voice, both audible and inaudible. We can hear the voice of the world through the vast amount of information from various media sources we encounter daily. We can hear the voices of others. We can hear the voice of evil from within as well as without. And we can hear the voice of God, primarily inaudible, but God has spoken audibly to some, also. Part of the problem we face is how to discern the different voices. We must be like the banking industry and learn how to determine what is real, as they do with currency, or money.

The biblical voice of God is our focus. The problem is to define authentically the voice of the Holy Spirit. Many readers will be willing to allow the Bible to be that standard, but what about those who disagree with that premise? Let us, like Abraham, not have a written standard. Let us lay down all written standards and allow our being to seek the One True Creator. See if you can hear Him in your daily experiences. If you need to read, you can read various sources for your research, but that must include the Bible. You can develop culture, principles, and philosophy to decide. But remember, the rules you apply to yourself must apply to everyone.

If, for example, tolerance is your value, then you must tolerate everything, even what you disagree with or deem wrong. If retribution is your standard, then you must take retribution on everyone equally, even those closest to you. If apathy is your rule, then you must be apathetic at all times, even toward subjects that you are passionate about. In other words, some standard must be established. If the Bible is your standard, then this is what one must use to become familiar with how God relates to humanity. To be fair,

Christians must lay aside all the doctrine they have amassed. As we learn His way of communication, all others will be recognized as counterfeit.

The God of the Bible does not say yes to everyone. He chastens and disciplines. He speaks truth that you actually experience. When I hear God's truth, I cannot argue with it. It is absolutely convincing. My voice, the voice of others, the voice of the enemy—all can be challenged. After a while, they are easily recognized and ignored. The voice of the Bible allows you to have a reference point. Dietrich Bonhoeffer said of the Bible, "You must inquire of it."[13]

Just as God speaks John-ish to me, the Bible helps each of us to hear God in our own language. From my reference point, the only voice of worth is God's voice. We must learn to recognize it within ourselves or when God uses another individual, situation, or event to help guide us. When you begin to get comfortable with His voice, you begin to trust Him. His song will fill your life. Unlike what religion teaches, the messages not directly meant for us are few and far between.

The voice of humankind always want us to judge others, to have a word for someone else's life. The not-God voices press us to share with those whom we believe need to hear it. The voice of God will always tell us we should heed first for ourselves what we hear. God is not interested in you and me fixing the world; He already did that. He is interested in fixing you and me. And in case you want to speak for God, remember this: to a person, men and women of God experienced a sense of fear and trepidation when they brought God's message to others.

Think about the lifespan of an individual who is recorded in the Bible. The writing is but a small portion of that time, some days or months only. If you combine all the writings of Paul, they could have been only a few months of events. Peter spent about three years with Jesus, and we have two small letters. Religion has taught people that we need to write a book a month. Some church celebrities make the body think that time would stop without their teachings. Yes, we are valuable to God, but we are just not that consistently valuable!

God made a way through His Son to cover our inconsistencies. Maybe we can help Him one percent of the time, so He can help us ninety-nine percent of the time. He sees our value in His Son. We must do the same and understand our value through Jesus, having the trust to know that our process, growth, and character is what He focuses on. Once again, I draw on a movie line from *The Matrix*. One character says to the other, "What was said was for you."[14] There goes Hollywood again. Those who listen carefully will find their life matures, grows, and flourishes in their relationship with God because we trust in His Son and hear that voice through the Holy Spirit. And maybe, just maybe, God may use us for a season to help His Kingdom.

The Most Intimate Act of Your Life

The Bible teaches that marriage is the relationship designed to give us the reality and the opportunity to understand what it means to be heard by another and to hear another, to care for another and have another care for you. So is child-rearing, but for the most part, it comes after the unity of two individuals. We have a basic need to want to be special to others. My wife works in a company that houses and cares for individuals with special needs and social disabilities. I believe we would all agree that these individuals are special, each one in their own way. But for a "normal" individual, it is almost comical to think about anyone "normal" being special. To be special to someone else takes quite a bit of effort. It takes a "bringing-in" of sorts.

Earlier I spoke about being alone. This bringing-in process is an attempt at not being alone, and it is at the discretion of the bringer-in. A common occurrence is a sort of confidante. We long to be that confidante or have that confidante. We develop friendships, some of which last a very long time, but many crash and burn. At heart we are unreliable. We see it in others, and others see it in us. This is why divorce is rampant and hurt is so prevalent. I am a conservative, Bible-teaching person, but I can understand why people find that relationship in the same sex and why the LGBTQ community exists.

I know many gays and lesbians who just want to be special, and they find that person within their own sex. I am not legitimizing biblically stated brokenness. I am delegitimizing brokenness that masquerades as "normal" in public while privately embracing this state of brokenness. We need to acknowledge our brokenness. No relationship between humans is perfect. But all are striving to experience being special. That experience comes not from love or sex; it comes from trust.

Intimacy is found in trust, not sexual unity. Rather, it stems from unity of being relevant, important, respected, desired, and loved. For any of those feelings to be realized, trust must make up the foundation of the individual. It is the most intimate act between two. The Greek word for trust is the same as faith. We tend to pigeon-hole the word *faith* and make it less relevant to our behavior because it is a religious word. Trust happens between individuals but not because of sex, talking, touching, meeting, holding, or the like. It occurs because both make an internal commitment that supersedes all other desires, wants, needs, and decisions.

One of the purposes of the Bible is to help us understand God. God demonstrates trust to us because His unity is trust. His unity is simply what defines it: One. We desire trust desperately. The problem is that without the Holy Spirit relationship, we can never mature in trust. God presents Himself over and over in relationships with individuals to help us develop a trust relationship with Him. The running theme for biblical personalities is that they trusted God. But this is a difficult concept to grasp because who can we trust?

The Bible for many is an outdated, mystical book that offers a tunnel-vison theme of peace and love. God revealed trust to me through my marital relationship. When I look into my wife's eyes, I realize she desires trust above all other things. Like many marriages, we have had disagreements. Every one of those times she required a response of trust, not necessarily agreement. Agreement always follows the trust portion of our relationship, even if we agree to disagree, but trust is paramount. Can you trust someone else with your body? Can you trust someone else with your child?

God chose Abraham because He trusted Abraham would teach His children about God. Today, Abraham still speaks trust through his life. We who trust Abraham are Abraham's children.

And Abraham's children are really God's children. Trust is so at our core that a broken trust is very difficult to regain, and at times it is simply impossible. "He who is faithful in a very little thing is faithful with very much; the one who is dishonest with very little is also dishonest with very much" (Luke 16:10 MW).

We can use this verse as a thermostat of sorts for our trust meter because trust approaches our borders for good and bad, right and wrong, valuable and worthless. Ask yourself if you can be trusted. Ask your enemies. Ask your friends. Ask the Holy Spirit. Intimacy begins in your trust.

The Spiritual Intimacy of God's Voice

In many ways, the Bible is a mystical book, or at least some feel it is. Maybe they are right, and if so, then those who hear from the Holy Spirit are also mystics. Maybe, hearing from God is just intimacy, just responsibility, and just trust.

Recently, I had an opportunity to better define this trust relationship. I am reminded of a verse that embodies my experience.

> The prophets sought and searched diligently concerning this salvation. They prophesied of the grace that would come to you. They were searching for what or what particular time the Spirit of Messiah which was in them was pointing to by testifying beforehand of the suffering of Messiah and the glories that would follow them. To them it was revealed that in these things, they were not serving themselves, but us. (1 Peter 1:10–12 MW)

The Holy Spirit spoke to me about a particular situation; let's say it was about fasting concerning a particular food when I had dinner with a friend who happened to be allergic to that food. Now fasting is something that I find very difficult. But my fasting would be for a reason and would produce a result whereby another individual in my life would be helped, maybe even grow to experience God's voice more clearly. I realized if I ate that food, I would be serving myself, but if I made it through my time of fasting, I would be serving the other. The question became this: Would I trust God on this issue? God loves and is always concerned about our growth and character. We should not ignore this principle when it comes to others hearing His voice.

Consider Hebrews, chapter 11, the pep-talk of all time. I get truth-bumps just reading it, which for me is one of the biblical tests for hearing God's voice. When I read it, truth covers me like a warm sweater on a cold day. I experience the voice of the Holy Spirit every time. In the chapter below, I have removed all the words *believe, faith* or *belief* and changed them to *trust*. See how it reads:

Now trust is the foundation of things hoped for, the certainty of things not seen. For those of older times obtained a good report by this. By trust, we understand that the ages were established by the spoken word of God, so that what is seen has not been made out of things which are visible. In trust, Abel offered to God a better sacrifice than Cain, through which he obtained confirmation that he was righteous – God testifying about his gifts. And through it, though having died, he still speaks. By trust Enoch was taken away, so that he would not see death. And he was not found, because God took him away, for it was testified of him before he was taken away that he pleased God. But apart from trust, it is impossible to please Him, for it is necessary that the one who comes to God trusts that He exists and that He is a rewarder of those who seek Him. In trust, Noah, being warned about things not yet seen, feared God and prepared and ark for the salvation of his house. By this he condemned the world, and became heir of the righteousness which is from trust. In trust, Abraham obeyed when he was called to go out to the place which he would receive for an inheritance. He went out, not knowing where he was going. In trust, he lived as a stranger in the promised land, as though foreign, dwelling in tents with Isaac and Jacob, the fellow heirs of the same promise. For he was awaiting the city which has foundation whose builder and framer is God. By trust when Sarah herself was barren and past the time of life, he received power to father a child, since he considered trustworthy the One who had promised. Therefore, also from one man, and him as good as dead, were born as many as the stars of the heaven in multitude and as innumerable as the sand which is by the shore of the sea. All these died in trust, not having received the promises, but having seen them and embraced them from a distance, and having confessed that they were foreigners and sojourners upon the land. For those who say such things make it clear that they are seeking their own homeland. If they truly had been remembering the one from which they went out, they would have had opportunity to return. However, as it is, they are searching for a better one, that from heaven. Therefore, God is not ashamed to be called their God; for He has prepared a city for them. Being tested, Abraham offered up Isaac in trust – he who had received the promises was offering up his only son. Since it was said about him, "In Isaac your seed will be called." He considered that God was able to raise him up, even from the dead. From there, figuratively speaking, he also received him back. In trust, Isaac blessed Jacob and Esau concerning things to come. By trust, Jacob, when he was dying, blessed each of the sons of Joseph and bowed down upon the top of his staff. By trust, Joseph, when his end was near, made mention of the exodus of the children of Israel, and gave instructions concerning his bones. When Moses was born, he was hidden for three months by his parents in trust, because they saw the child was good, and they were not afraid of the king's command. When Moses had grown up, in trust he refused to be called the son of Pharaohs daughter, choosing to suffer affliction with Gods people rather than to have the temporary enjoyment of sin. He considered the disgrace of the Messiah to be greater riches that the treasures of Egypt, because he looked to the reward. In trust, he left Egypt, not fearing the anger of the king, because he persevered while seeing the invisible. In trust he kept the Passover and the sprinkling of the blood, so that the destroyer of the firstborn could not touch them. By trust, they passed through the Red Sea as on dry land. When the Egyptians tried to do so they were swallowed up. By trust the walls of Jericho fell down, after they had been encircled for seven days. By trust Rahab the harlot, having received the spies in peace, did not perish with those who were disobedient. What more shall I say? For the time would fail me if I spoke about Gideon, Barak, Samson, Yiftah, David, Samuel, and the prophets. Through trust they conquered kingdoms, did works of righteousness, attained promises, stopped the mouths of lions, extinguished the power of fire, escaped the edge of the sward, were make strong form weakness, became mighty in war and routed foreign armies. Women receive their dead raised to life. Yet other were tortured, not receiving their deliverance, so that they might obtain a better resurrection. Still others underwent testing by mocking and whipping, and by chains and imprisonment beyond that. They were stoned. They were sawn apart. They were tempted. They were slaughtered with the sward. They went around in sheepskins, in goatskins, being destitute, afflicted, mistreated. The wandered in deserts, mountains, caves, and holes of the earth. The world was not worthy of them. But all these, their trust testifying of them did not receive the promise. God having foreseen something better for us, so that they should not receive fulfillment apart from us. (Heb 11:-1-40 MW)

These individuals all experienced intimacy with God. They saw that what they were enduring was for us, not for them. Intimacy with God is an experience that one wants others to have. Hebrews 11 is an example of why the Bible trains us to hear His voice. The Bible speaks of this spiritual connection, of unity and oneness with God. God is One, and trust is established in Him. But betrayal, or broken trust, occurs in many ways, and humanity is replete with it. It can happen in relationships, such as marriages, business partnerships, financial agreements, families, politics, and more. The reason it is so devastating is that it affects the spiritual part of us, the depths of the human being: our intimacy and our trust. The most intimate act that can occur between two beings is trust; the most consequential is the breaking of trust.

You might be tempted to think otherwise, so let us speak of a few acts that masquerade as intimacy. Words can be mistaken for a bond of trust. In our day and age, phrases such as "I love you" or "trust me" have lost their power and meaning. Physical contact, such as a handshake, has lost its promise. Actions, such as a kiss, a hug, or hand holding mean different things to men and women. Women holding hands with a loved one while walking at the mall may be thinking, "Everyone, especially other women, can see how much we are connected and in love." Men are thinking, "I hope no one, especially my guy friends, sees me," or "If I do this silliness now, it should count for getting sex later."

Physical contact is not a sign of trust. Neither is sex. Sex is usually the first thought on people's minds when asked the question about intimacy, but a quick ten seconds and most people, especially older ones, blow this off with a chuckle. Anyone who has experienced physical intimacy can realize both how beautiful and how empty it can be. So, why are some people devastated when after giving their most private experience to another person, that other person walks away or commits the same act with someone else? It is because they feel betrayed. The other person has trampled a trust—intimacy.

The sad part is that most of the time both, yes both, of the individuals simply did not understand that the offer was for trust, not sex. Sex was just the vehicle. This is why intercourse is not just a physical joining. The participants have actually made a spiritual bond because they have given away something that they cannot get back, which is trust. Unfortunately, the act of sex is not a bond of trust; it is an attempt at trust, which is unseen.

On the other hand, the bond of trust can lead to many an experience that fulfills an individual. Therefore, there is much more to the fulfillment of trust between two individuals than a physical connection. Intimacy, or trust, occurs between individuals. The movie

Jerry McGuire has a line of great significance when it comes to trust when Jerry said, "You complete me" [15]

Intimacy is more than a hug, a thought, or a word. It is more than a look, a hand held, a smile, or a kiss. Human has betrayed human with each one of these. Trust is developed over time; it resides below the skin level, yet it can be *recognized in a moment.* Trust recognition begins with learning that *we* can be trustworthy. This begins to lay the tracks for a journey that has wonderful implications. If one attempts to understand the magnitude of trust, their journey has its foundations in the relationship with the Holy Spirit and Jesus. Intimacy is achieved when two become one in trust, and they are unmoved in this relationship for life. Trustworthiness and intimacy are taught by God. Jesus could and can be trusted. He is the example of trust.

> Do not let your heart be troubled; trust in God, trust also in me. In my Father's house are many dwellings. If it were not so, I would have told you, because I am going to prepare a place for you. (John 14:1–2 MW)

God's voice will help you love God and Jesus His Son. His voice will teach you that Jesus is the center of the universe; everything depends on Him and all good comes from Him. He will teach you how to be trustworthy. God's voice will guide you to learn selflessness, so you can be trusted by others and trust yourself. God's voice will help you to be compassionate and merciful. God's voice will allow you to see the weakness and frailty of the human condition, even that of arrogant and merciless humans.

God's voice will teach patience, and then it will teach you more patience. God's voice will teach you humility. God's voice will help you to forgive others. God's voice will guide you to judge yourself and then to forgive yourself, especially for not obeying His voice. God's voice will wake you up and help you sleep. God's voice will become the voice of the Holy Spirit. God's voice will teach you to love without defining the word because you cannot define it. You can only *be* love.

God's voice will not teach you to hate. God's voice will not teach you to hurt others. God's voice will not teach you to judge others devoid of forgiveness. God's voice will teach you to fear the absence of God's presence, which is, in and of itself, punishment. God's voice will teach you to pray and pray and pray. Then it will teach you the power of prayer and teach you to pray more. It is a small whisper that you cannot distance yourself from once you hear it because you know that distancing yourself will only leave you empty and alone. Aloneness, which we spoke about earlier, is the state you came from and really don't want to return to.

When I was a younger man and heard the voice of God, I inevitably mixed it with the voice of the world, in my case religion, and thought the voice was there so I could tell others what God said. This is a foundational problem faced by humanity. There is a lot of static, especially our own brokenness, which prevents us from actually hearing His voice. Jesus would often say, "To the one who has ears, let him hear." Obviously we all have ears. But those organs must also function. We must also care. Function is important when tuning in to the voice of God. Notice I say "tuning." This is a constant process—not because God has different channels but because we like listening to other channels. Therefore, we must retune daily.

As I mentioned earlier, the problem with organizational religion is that we think we know some things that we really are clueless about. The canon of the Bible are recordings of and about men and women who heard from God. We are wrongly taught that what we read was some type of constant state of being tuned in. This is not accurate; it was a journey. Take Peter, for example. Paul called him out for acting with hypocrisy toward Gentiles years after the resurrection. No, these are glimpses into the lives of people who heard God's voice. I have calculated that we have a record, in total, of Jesus for about four weeks of His entire life over some thirty-three years. The glimpse of life for each writer might span, as in the case of Moses, one hundred and twenty years, but what is recorded was over only a matter of weeks, months, or just a few years of their lives. Our perspective is skewed because we apply those glimpses to our lives and think hearing from God is a smooth road of constant bliss. No, the moment-by-moment voice is for our own journey. It is to make us more Godly, and that by God's standards, not an organization's and certainly not our own.

Prayer

Prayer is a controversial topic. The reason is because this religious concept is universal in terms of commonality but is splintered in terms of religion. I claim there is only one God. I have identified my Deity clearly in this writing. The entire theme of this book is relationship with Him, hearing from Him, and speaking to Him—in a word, prayer.

I have friends who participate in both Christian and non-Christian religions. In many conversations, people consistently express the thought that prayer is a request. They claim they expect a response. They also claim that their requests are prioritized, so to speak. For example, they may pray for a healing, but they probably will not pray for a new bicycle for their child. Desperation and need clearly determine their prioritization, urgency, and frequency. This writing attempts to explain that prayer is talking to and hearing from God. I am challenged by one-sided prayer. God speaking to us—I mean really communicating on a regular basis—is foreign to humans. You would think that we want to hear from God. This is not the reality. In the time of *Moses, the people did not want to hear God's voice. It scared them. So they opted for a representative, who was Moses.

Sometimes God's voice brings fear on me, also. But God is not one-dimensional. He also brings us love. Dating back to Moses, the norm for religion is that someone else hears for us. All religion has a hierarchical group who interprets for them. God wants to communicate with each person; He has said it and has demonstrated it by the presence of His Holy Spirit. There are likely many skeptics. One of my maxims as a young believer was, "I am not called to prayer." Never say never! While I have focused time to present needs to God in a specific timeframe, I am constantly interacting (praying) with the Holy Spirit.

Our communication with God can involve several levels of processes and dimensions. We can pray formal, repetitive-type prayers.

We can yell and grunt and speak in tongues. We can simply talk to God in the same manner as we speak to other people. We can ask questions. We can communicate audibly and inaudibly. We can wait on Him. We can reason with God. After all, He is very reasonable, and as I have found out, He is much more reasonable than I am. If you decide to reason with Him, be prepared to be reasoned into His way because hearing truth is very convincing. You see, I have found out that God cannot be manipulated, so losing a difference of opinion will become a normal occurrence. He knows better. And if you let Him, He will make you better.

I am persuaded in my prayer life to pray five areas of Scripture as rote or redundant prayers. They are the prayer of Jabez, the Shema, the Our Father, Psalm 23 and The Ten Commandments. I have chosen these because they functionally cover areas of God's Word that I need to be reminded of daily. They also remind me of concepts that I need to review daily. These are my choices as guided by the Holy Spirit. I encourage you to pray any Scripture you desire.

I invoke God's will and discipline in my life. I have given God license to chastise and teach me. I have asked Him to change me into a better decision maker. In fact, I have told my children for years that being a good decision maker is one of my major desires for them, maybe the most important. I ask God to watch over our spirits, souls, and bodies. I ask for God to dispatch angels to protect us and others, to watch over our thoughts and emotions, and to secure our finances. I ask God to help His family here on earth and bring about His Kingdom, to help the persecuted all over the globe, and to help people who have good lives to continually submit prayers at the foot of His throne for all worldwide needs. There is more I pray for, but this list is sufficient for now.

On the converse side, God has directed me in many ways. You see, God wants to communicate with us. When I look back at my younger self, the best description I have is that I was a pompous ass. I directed my older siblings and their spouses, who had children, about the best way to raise those children, even though I did not have children. Fortunately for me, they are gracious people. God made me apologize in writing. I have many memories, some of which remind me of my failing moments. One day, through a video called *An Interview with God* [16] God helped me to understand that I must forgive myself for my failures and to remember that He has. This realization brought on many tears caused by years of regret and reminders of failure. I still fail and make bad decisions, and God still meets with me and prays with me. The Holy Spirit directs me in those prayers and brings me through each day.

Worship and Music

Here is what Jesus said about worship:

> You worship that which you do not know; we worship that which we know, for salvation is from the Jews. But an hour is coming, and now is, when those truly submitted shall worship the Father in spirit and truth; for such people the Father seeks to be His worshipers. God is spirit, and those who worship Him must worship in spirit and truth. (John 4:22–24 MW)

The word *worship* in this verse is the same as any other verse in the Greek. It simply means to be submitted. I personally have sung many songs in church, in my car, on runs, while exercising, and more. Somehow, I never realized that singing and worship are two different words and maybe two different activities. I showed up Sunday morning to worship, but I rarely did. This is because I did not like the songs, was distracted by the worship team's clothing, mannerisms, types of instruments, by other congregants, by how I saw the manner in which other people "worshipped," by the use of banners, and more. I understand that I am broken and that my readers may not have any of these issues, but I will continue on with the topic.

I was not worshipping because I was not submitted at the moment of singing. Oh, I had many a Sunday morning where charisma was present, my charisma. I was filled with emotions, laughed, cried, stood up, went down, and more. But there was, for many years, a void. I figured if I looked like or acted like other congregation members, I was worshipping. In the verse mentioned above, Jesus's words, "God is Spirit," are central. He did not say anything about singing, raising hands, clapping, being happy, or feeling sad, or any of the other physical or emotional hooks we experience in today's contemporary services. I thought we worshipped on Sunday morning at church, but God did not even say anything about getting together on Sunday to worship. My concept of worship was broken. I think it bordered on the cultic.

The Holy Spirit began to help me understand that worship is about submission. The Greek word, as mentioned earlier, speaks of bowing down. This concept comes from *TaNaKh,* better known as the Old Testament. In my relationship with the Holy Spirit, I began to learn that one worships God when submitted at that very moment of spiritual interaction, such as allowing the Holy Spirit to quell your frustration or anger, to communicate respectfully to others, and to be patient. The spirit of the individual must bow before or submit to the indwelling Spirit of God. I began to realize that worship was not limited to song. I allowed the Holy Spirit to be present in my thought life, moment by moment. My thoughts must yield to the Holy Spirit's leading. Paul said it this way: "throwing down calculated plans and every high thing that exalts itself against the knowledge of God, and bringing every thought into captivity to the obedience of the Messiah." (2 Corinthians 10:5 MW).

We must control our thoughts and yield them to the Creator of our spirits. The mind must surrender to the principles of the Holy Spirit and God's Word. When God was finally able to free me from the bondage of what I thought was worship, I began to interact with the Holy Spirit during music performed in a church in a corporate way. Today the people around me fade away. Yet, I can roll a car to my grandson or mind my granddaughter at the same time. Fading away does not mean my surroundings disappear. It simply means that the Holy Spirit has His hook in me, and nothing I do distracts me from that time.

My standard is not how I think or how an organization conceives worship should happen. It is what God wants to happen. What God wants is for Him to be the focus. I don't have to be alone with Him. I just need to know He is the company for my aloneness. This is spirit-worship, the kind that Jesus spoke about. I go to service and sing. This is a great blessing, and I encourage you to sing, also.

I also encourage you to worship. I love bowing my spirit to God in my daily decision-making that I do in worship. When I was not worshipping, I was bowing my spirit to my thoughts and distractions. Jesus's reference above is the process whereby the inside "something" of a person yields to someone "other" than themselves, offering reverence. Humankind, over the millennia, has worshipped a variety of things, such as rocks, mountains, planets, people, animals, dead people, or just about any created thing, and, yes, intangible gods. How does one demonstrate reverence toward the one true God? Having reverence indicates approaching Him with deep respect or regard. So, if you put this all together, you can actually evaluate who or what you worship.

Let's say a famous personality, like a Hollywood star or a celebrated politician, walks into your workplace. How do you act? You treat that person with reverence. You yield to his or her presence. So, in order to worship in spirit, one must regard God the Spirit with reverence, a reverence that begins in our own spirit and expands to mind and body. You have never seen God the Spirit. How do you recognize Him? You are not even sure if you can interact with Him—but you can. This occurs by yielding or bowing our spirit to the Creator, which allows us to acquiesce to godly thoughts during our daily activities. The ungodly ones will have no hold on you.

An attempt must be made and a process developed to capture daily our thoughts and yield them to examination by the Holy Spirit, who will yea or nay them. This vital step is what is missing in religion. Because of a lack of connection to the Holy Spirit, we have seen, through the veil of religion, some of the vilest acts perpetrated by people throughout history based on worship of their gods. Human and demonic forces have perverted God's design for relationship and service. But that does not mean *we* cannot yield to God in spirit. That does not mean that you cannot yield to God in a way that worships Him with every thought that emanates from within you, and by the way, sing, sing, sing!

Compassion and Mercy

> Having then a great High Priest who has passed through the heavens, Jesus the Son of God, let us hold tightly to our commitment. For we do not have a High Priest who cannot sympathize with our weaknesses, but one who has likewise been tempted in all things, yet without sin. Let us therefore approach the throne of grace with boldness, so that we may receive mercy, and my find grace for timely help. (Heb 4:14–1 MW)

One of the problems we run into in life is the mindset of "you cannot understand what I am going through" or "you don't know how I feel." When you hear yourself or someone else say these types of statements, a big red flag should go up in your mind. Humanity, because of aloneness, wants, at times, to exist in a place where we cannot be reached. Aloneness is a love/hate relationship. We hate being alone, so we use it to our advantage. This manipulation actually began through demonic influence, but humanity has embraced it.

Adam in essence said to God, "You don't know how I feel; you cannot relate to me." And of course, God knows everything, so He knew exactly what Adam felt. We want our hurt to be unreachable by others who don't agree with us. This attitude keeps us safe within our box of hurt. Race, ethnic, and religious relations are at low points in our society today because of this thought process. Depression and other physical and psychological medical conditions have debilitated our society as a result. Massive dysfunction is fueled by this weakness. Yes, it is a symptom of human weakness, a feebleness that we hold onto with a passion, without even realizing it.

Just think about how often people complain. We whine over how sick we are or how many doctors we need to visit. We complain about politics, finances, food, and more. We socialize on these topics ad nauseam. Human frailty, aloneness, and brokenness are behind all that ails us. Let's look at a few examples of what I call "the human factor," a condition that affects everyone.

The church, at large, suffers from this disease. Its leaders love to call out sin. They want to make sure the world knows they are speaking for God with their words. The problem is human weakness. Some of their pet subjects are abortion, homosexuality, lesbianism, and evolution. This is not necessarily about who people are but about what they do. Jesus spent most of His time praying for people. Jesus spent most of His time healing people. Jesus spent most of His time teaching people. He focused on who people were, as He does today. Even the woman caught in prostitution was dispensed compassion.

> Jesus straightened up and asked her, "Woman, where are they? Has no one condemned you?" "No one, sir," she said. "Then neither do I condemn you," Jesus declared. "Go now and leave your life of sin." (John 8:10–11 NIV)

He addressed her brokenness with compassion. He addressed her as who she was, not what she did. Crowds came to Him because He had compassion. Compassion resulted in action. He also has love, but love, in our language, is not necessarily a word of action, so I prefer the word *compassion* to be the filter we use to respond to life. In the church today, people initially come because of Jesus, but as time goes on, Jesus gets obscured. They can't see Jesus anymore. Jesus has become like the Christmas tree. We have hung so many decorations, such as ministries, doctrines, rules, and regulations, on Him that He is not clearly visible anymore. Therefore, people burn out and fall away. They never get to Jesus Himself because the church leaders don't let them get to Him. By the way, this is not something new:

> "Woe to you Torah Scholars, Perushim, pretenders! For you shut up heavens kingdom in front of the people! But you do not enter in and you do not permit those who are entering to enter. "Woe to you Torah Scholars and Perushim, pretenders! For you travel around by sea and land to make one proselyte; and when he becomes one, you make him

twice as much a son of Gehinnom as yourselves!" (Mathew 23:13–15 MW)

So, how do we change? Part of the problem is that love, as a filter, can be problematic. We can claim we love someone as a mental exercise but never actually convert it into actions. Our words are not empowered, or they are empowered by deception. One example is the topic of sex. Sexual deviation is a large problem that is mostly focused on homosexuality and lesbianism. But it exists in heterosexual relationships, also.

I have found that one of our greatest areas of brokenness surrounds sex. The argument that is made to legitimize homosexuality is that it is not a choice; people were born that way. Is this possible? My answer is yes, not to legitimacy but to being born a particular way, broken. My reason is that society has taken other issues, such as body image and size bias, and accepted it as an inborn characteristic. In modern society, people have fought to be thin until size bias has become a topic. The inborn battle of an individual about size is similar to sexual orientation, depression, and other emotional challenges.

There are many indwelling issues that plague the human psyche, including virility and femininity, as well as physical beauty and inward grace. What about pedophilia? Were people born like that? How about being a bully? Is it possible for people to be born like that? How about violence? My sons played football for years, and I found myself rooting for them to take down their opponents. I deluded myself by thinking that I really did not want them to hurt another player, but come on, it is a violent game, and violence is going to take place, even in the minds of parents. I say it is all possible, and that we are born this way—broken! We can't see it because it is like being born and living under water. One cannot imagine what it would be like to breathe air.

Human frailty is about brokenness. The issue is nonconformity to God's plan; I don't like to use the word *sin* anymore, so brokenness is our nature. We are consigned to this futility by choice, but we were also consigned in hope:

For the creation was subjected to futility, not of its own will, but because of the One who subjected it, in hope that the creation itself also will be delivered from the bondage of decay into the liberty of the glory of the children of God. (Romans 8:20–21 MW)

God wants us to overcome our brokenness and the futility we live in. The problem is we continually are trying to overcome it through our own strength. God wants us to go to Him for help. The most significant moment in my life is when I forgave myself for my bad decisions, my brokenness. I was about forty years old. My office is littered with my failures. You would think that it would be adorned with achievements, like more "normal" people. There are some, but I kept the failures to remember. And boy, did I.

I reminded myself daily of mistakes. It took me years to forgive myself for walking out of my father's nursing home the day he developed pneumonia. Two weeks later, he passed away. I never had the chance for another conversation with him. The day before he died I wept as I gave him his last shave. Even in his unconscious state his reflexes let me shave under his nose. It was almost like he was with me. So, I needed to exercise compassion on myself first. This is how God begins to fix brokenness. Compassion is a godly attribute, foreign to humanity. After that, I exercised compassion on others. Overcoming is not possible without compassion, and compassion is not possible without God's help. It was the Holy Spirit who gave me the knowledge, wisdom, and strength to be compassionate. Without the Holy Spirit, true compassion does not exist. Compassion begins with forgiving ourselves, and forgiveness is not possible without Jesus.

Give God a Chance

I had a conversation with my sister-in-law about the lens through which we see ourselves. People may ask God, why did you make me this way? (We do ask these types of questions.) And if we ask it, that means in some way we are not happy about our brokenness. By the way, our brokenness drills down to the depths of our being. I find I like going there, but the journey is slow and arduous. If you are unhappy about something in yourself, then you must seek a lens through which you can view this to attain joy. The best answer is to look through the lens of the Holy Spirit.

The result is attaining your feeling of approval from God. Self-approval or human approval is never enough. The only one who counts is Jesus. He has a most powerful lens that removes human-kind's visual distortion, an enormous struggle. And the really neat part of this plan is that God's approval comes in one way—through the grace of Jesus the Messiah. You don't work for it. There is nothing you can do to earn it. Your being's fullness can only be achieved by trust, not actions. That trust is all God wants. Look at what trust did for Abraham:

> And Abraham stretched out his hand, and took the knife to slay his son.

> But the angel of the LORD called to him from heaven, and said, "Abraham, Abraham!" And he said, "Here I am." And he said, "Do not stretch out your hand against the lad, and do nothing to him; for now I know that you fear God, since you have not withheld your son, your only son, from Me."

> Then Abraham raised his eyes and looked, and behold, behind *him* a ram caught in the thicket by his horns; and Abraham went and took the ram, and offered him up for a burnt offering in the place of his son. And Abraham called the name of that place The LORD Will Provide, as it is said to this day, "In the mount of the LORD it will be provided." Then the angel of the LORD called to Abraham a second time from heaven, and said, "By Myself I have sworn, declares the LORD, because you have done this thing, and have not withheld your son, your only son, indeed I will greatly bless you, and I will greatly multiply your seed as the stars of the heavens, and as the sand which is on the seashore; and your seed shall possess the gate of their ene-mies. "And in your seed all the nations of the earth shall

be blessed, because you have obeyed My voice." (Genesis 22:10–18 NASB)

Abraham trusted God enough to offer up Isaac. God promised his posterity blessing. He did it. God trusted us enough to offer up His Son Jesus. He knew some would find their hope in Him. Jesus is the answer to the brokenness of humankind because He will dispense the Holy Spirit. Will you trust Him to speak to you and heal your brokenness? Give God the chance.

The Father's Promise to His Son

As a parent, I have experienced both thoughts and events concerning my children. The one universal piece of advice I give new parents is that your child will make you see parts of yourself that you never dreamed existed. Do not miss that opportunity to learn about yourself. When a life is born, parents see hope that we hold onto for years as our child grows. In our minds, we see greatness. As time goes on, we learn that our child has the same weaknesses as is common to humanity. Parents of children with disabilities see this relatively quickly. The more talented or gifted an individual is, the longer it takes or the more difficult it is to recognize this frailty. By the time a parent recognizes this weakness, some are motivated to plan. In the case of a rich person, the offspring may get a position of security in the family business. For the vast majority of people, it may range from planning for college to living in a group home with others of similar circumstances.

Parents have a responsibility. They may not live up to it, but it exists in every case. God, the ultimate parent, expresses His responsibility in many ways and through a host of biblical events, specifically in the account of Abraham. We don't give Abraham enough attention in our readings, but this was an individual in whom God was very interested—not because God needed to learn about Abraham but because Abraham needed to learn about Abraham. Abraham desired to be an intimate friend of God, and God with Abraham. In a previous Scripture, God promised Abraham that He

99

would provide for him and his posterity. The Holy Spirit communicated it through Moses for us to read.

The Bible is replete with accounts of the responsibility that God exercises. This is because the Father made a promise to His Son. God wants you and me, His children, to take hold of His example of responsibility. He wants us to draw on the Holy Spirit for strength, wisdom, and courage to be responsible. God promised us responsibility millennia ago and fulfilled that promise by His Son Jesus. Some parents see their responsibility as inherited from their heavenly Father and communicated through the voice of the Holy Spirit. Ask the Holy Spirit to help you desire the same.

How Much Can We Know about God?

> He also spoke a parable to them that they should always pray and not give up. He said, "there was a judge in certain city who did not fear God, and did not respect man. There was a widow in that city who often came to him saying, "give me justice against my opponent!" For some time, he would not, but afterward he would say to himself, "Though I neither fear God nor respect man, yet because this widow bothers me, I will give her justice, so that she doesn't wear me out by her continued coming." The Lord said, "Listen to what the unrighteous judge said. Will not God execute justice for his chosen who are crying out day and night? I tell you He will execute justice for them speedily. Never the less, when the Son of Adam comes will he find faith on the earth?" (Luke 18:1-8 MW)

The above passage is a typical biblical parable that demonstrates how God reasons differently than humans. The problem is that, as a human, I sometimes really don't understand how other people reason, and I know that they have the same confusion about my reasoning. Additionally, I don't understand how I reason in certain situations, so how can I possibly understand how God reasons? There is much that goes into how we think cognitively about something.

We may or may not feel emotion. We may have physical symptoms about a situation. Our entire being—spirit, soul, and body—can all get involved, leaving us with a host of thoughts, symptoms, and feelings that drive us in one direction or another. Look at the judge in the parable above, whose cognitive thinking was influenced by emotional or physical considerations of being worn out.

It is important to realize that our entire being, whatever that is made of, is involved in our reasoning process. If this is true for us, it should be true for God, but on a much more complex level because we are made in His image. Since we are like Him, let me dissect one point from the above parable that often leads us to believe that God is like us. The judge made a decision based on his level of frustration. Jesus was telling us that God would also make a decision, but we can conclude that it will be based on love, compassion, mercy, and more, not because of brokenness. This following verse lists God the Spirit's effects: "²² But the fruit of the Spirit is love, joy, peace, patient endurance, kindness, goodness, faithfulness, ²³ gentleness, self-control; against such things no law exists." (Galatians 5:22–23 MW).

These are the basis of God's decision-making. He puts all of these in His decision-making, and He wants us to experience them so we can incorporate them into our decision-making process. If we had infinite wisdom, then we would not get frustrated, and hence, we would make good decisions like God. However, we have the next best option, the Holy Spirit. When we find ourselves gravitating to these qualities, we can be sure we are hearing from the Holy Spirit. So, we are given an example of how God makes decisions and provision for us. Is it possible for us to conceive how God, a perfect being, does actually make decisions? Ask Him! "If you then, though you are evil, know how to give good gifts to your children, how much more will your Father in heaven give the Holy Spirit to those who ask him" (Luke 11:13 NIV)!

Unity, Not Unit

As stated earlier, intimacy is about trust. For trust to work between two individuals, we must first trust ourselves. We must learn a personal intimacy that reveals to ourselves who we are inside. The world offers many reasons for us to berate ourselves over a host of issues, such as appearance, job performance, social standing, and relationships. With these concerns, we fight the fact that we question the matter of self-trust. You may say, "That is preposterous; I can trust myself." Or, you may be unsure. Either way we all have experienced times when we wanted to grab our words in midair before they hit the ears of the hearer.

We may have had times when we have hurt loved ones and wished we could take back our words. In the world of email and Twitter, we may have had times where we wanted to recall the messages, but it was too late. Trusting oneself begins with being a law-abiding citizen in the Kingdom of God—the Kingdom established within oneself. A relationship with the Holy Spirit offers us the ability to change what ails us, not conceal it. This relationship demonstrates that the answer to our emotional challenges is not found in the next prescription bottle we pick up at the pharmacy.

God understands trust. It must be present in our inner being before it can occur between two. This is why God refers to Himself as *Echad* in the Hebrew, which means Unity. God's unity is One. Each individual that represents the Unity understands and practices trust and intimacy. God the Holy Spirit can teach each of us about personal unity, and if all practiced unity, trust, and valued intimacy, then we would choose many of our words differently. We would view others through the lens of compassion, and we would walk humbly. Our unit would live in unity—spirit, soul, and body. Here are several passages that embody the results of this principle.

> You shall not take vengeance, nor bear any grudge against the sons of your people, but you shall love your neighbor as yourself; I am the LORD. (Leviticus 19:18 NASB)

> He has shown you, O mortal, what is good. And what does the LORD require of you? To act justly and to love mercy and to walk humbly with your God. (Micah 6:8 NIV)

Behold, as for the proud one, His soul is not right within him; But the righteous will live by his faith (trust). (Habakuk 2:4 NASB)

These verses are powerful and meaningful toward the maturity of a person's unit being unified. The last verse above not only speaks to the benefit of trust but also validates the negative effects on the soul when one does not walk in personal unity, which cannot be accomplished without the counsel of the Most High, the Holy One of Israel. God is the answer for what ails you, beginning with the need for personal unity, internal trust.

We're Up Here and You're Down There!

Humans are enamored with the idea of authority. We want to be the authority, but we are acutely aware that in reality there is some authority over us: parents, bosses, government, and God. So, if we must acquiesce to this situation, we would like to choose who that authority over us is. This goes back millennia.

Then all the elders of Israel gathered together and came to Samuel at Ramah; and they said to him, "Behold, you have grown old, and your sons do not walk in your ways. Now appoint a king for us to judge us like all the nations." But the thing was displeasing in the sight of Samuel when they said, "Give us a king to judge us." And Samuel prayed to the LORD. And the LORD said to Samuel, "Listen to the voice of the people in regard to all that they say to you, for they have not rejected you, but they have rejected Me from being king over them." (1Samuel 8:4–7 NASB)

16 This is according to all that you asked of the LORD your God in Horeb on the day of the assembly, saying, "Let me not hear again the voice of the LORD my God, let me not see this great fire anymore, lest I die." And the LORD said to me, "They have spoken well. 'I will raise up a prophet from among their countrymen like you, and I will put My words in

his mouth, and he shall speak to them all that I command him."
(Deu 18:16–18 NASB)

Jesus the Nazarene, a man attested to you by God with mir-
acles and wonders and signs which God performed through
Him in your midst, just as you yourselves know — this *Man*,
delivered up by the predetermined plan and foreknowledge
of God, you nailed to a cross by the hands of godless men
and put *Him* to death. (Acts 2:22–23 NASB)

Sometimes, human choice of earthly authority is done out of
fear. Other times — no, I believe every time — it is done out of fear,
and this includes voting in a democracy. One of my favorite movies
is *The Rock*. In one scene, Ed Harris, who is speaking to a group of
elite SEALs, says, "We're up here and you're down there"[17] ! He
was making them aware that he and his men had the upper hand
because their position was physically elevated over the others. This
is a military principle, and his line is meant to demonstrate advantage, superiority, and authority. The SEALs, in the lower position,
decided not to give authority to the group above them, and hence
they were killed.

Who has authority when it comes to biblical interpretation and
explanation? Authority is a funny phenomenon. It can be personal.
If you were to speak to my aunt about making meatballs, she would
clearly say she is the authority. We have Iron Chefs today, who are
viewed as authorities in cooking. They have experiential knowledge, probably more than my aunt, but are they really *the* authorities? I understand meatballs and cooking are subjective, but I'm
hungry and near the end of my writing. Let's move on.

Authority can be logical. I am a pharmacist. I have seen two
medical experts, physicians, completely disagree as to the cause
of my wife's symptoms in her visit to the emergency room. Who
was the authority? They both had knowledge, but that did not make
them the ultimate authority. They logically concluded their opinions. Real authority is an absolute, and the conclusion is absolute.
The authority of doctors making a physical medical diagnosis is

problematic in many cases until the results come in by a higher authority, such as an MRI.

How about emotional diagnoses? Remember how much the problem of aloneness affects the physical. Every day we look to media devices to find some piece of information that fills our desire for ultimate authority. Each of us chooses our authority, what or who we decide will be over us. Today, the media leads society around with a nose ring. The talking heads parade "experts" on every channel, convincing the undiscriminating mind that they can be relied upon for accurate information. Authority is the power to influence or command thought, opinion, or behavior. The media has it where humans are concerned. This media is the organization represented in Revelation 13:11.

The voice of the Holy Spirit is ridiculed by the secular. In some cases, it is manipulated by organized religion. In the case of the Bible, we individuals who study it have authority to some degree. But just like the physicians in the ER, we stand toe to toe and disagree when given the same set of verses. We are highly protective of our results. We create brick houses of doctrines secured with the cement of Bible verses and build until they reach the sky. Jesus spoke about corrupt leadership:

And He said to them, "You are those who in the sight of men declare yourselves righteous, but God knows your hearts. For what is exalted among men is an abomination in the sight of God." (Luke 16:15 MW)

But the Bible tells us He, the Holy Spirit, will be with us and live in us. "But the Helper, the Holy Spirit, whom the Father will send in My name, He will teach you all things, and bring to your remembrance all that I said to you" (John 14:26 NASB).

And God continues to scatter us like chaff in the wind in the hope that some of us will realize that "we're down here, and He is up there!"

THE GREATEST HOME COURT ADVANTAGE OF ALL TIME!

God Has a Plan

The movie, *The American President,* includes a line similar to the heading of this section. Michael Douglas (as the US President) says, "The White House is the single greatest home court advantage in the modern world" [18]

God's people, through Jesus, have been given the single greatest home court advantage of all time. The presence of the Holy Spirit is how we experience intimacy with God, with true compassion and forgiveness. Hearing and communicating with God occurs because of the Holy Spirit's indwelling. The Bible is replete with these interactions. In fact, the Bible even depicts interactions between God's Spirit and ungodly individuals, such as Balaam and Caiaphas. God will use who He will use to keep His promise to His children. And it is the presence of the Holy Spirit that brings true victory. Within the human framework throughout time, people view victory in different ways. Financial success is one way. Power is another. When combined, they produce within the human an eternally deadly result. But the Bible suggests solutions:

> When pride comes, then comes dishonor, But with the humble is wisdom. (Pro 11:2 NASB)

> but God has chosen the foolish things of the world so that He might put to shame those that are wise. God has chosen the weak things of this world so that he might put to shame those which are strong. (1 Corinthians 1:27 MW)

Therefore I think it is good to be in weakness, in inju-
ries, in sufferings, in persecutions, in distresses for
Messiah. For whenever I am weak then I am powerful. (2
Corinthians 12:10 MW)

These are not embraced by humans unless the Spirit of God is
living in them. The presence of the Spirit was promised by Jesus
and is recognized by the believer.

Nevertheless, I tell you the truth, it is to your benefit that I
go away. For if I do not go away, the Advocate will not come
to you. But if I go, I will send Him to you. When He has
come, He will rebuke the world concerning sin, concerning
righteousness and concerning judgement. Concerning sin,
because they do not believe in me; concerning righteousness, because I am going to my Father and you will not see
me anymore; concerning judgement, because the ruler of
this world has been judged.

"I still have many things to tell to you, but you cannot hear
them now. "However, when He, the Spirit of truth, has
come, *He will guide you* into all the truth because He will
not speak from Himself. He will speak instead whatever
He hears. He will declare to you what is coming. "He shall
glorify Me; for He shall take of Mine, and shall declare *it*
to you. "Everything that the Father has are Mine. Therefore
I said, that He takes of Mine, and will declare *it* to you."
(John 16:7–15 MW; bolding is my emphasis)

"If you love Me, you will keep My commandments. "I will
ask the Father, and He will give you another Advocate, so
that He may be with you forever - The Spirit of truth, whom
the world cannot receive, because it neither sees Him nor
knows Him. You know Him because He lives with you, and
will be in you." (John 14:15–17 MW)

This is our advantage and our strength. He is our best friend and connects us to the center of the universe. Jesus is the Messiah; He is the Life—our life. We exist in Him. Everything exists in Him. All who come to Him find God the Father. The Holy Spirit has revealed them to us, and we are playing on our home court when we allow the Holy Spirit to change us into Kingdom citizens working for the Kingdom that will endure forever. Will you let Him guide you?

Stop and listen carefully, for it is the single most important action you will ever take, one that will fill your present life with meaning and open the door to intimacy, unity, and eternal life in the presence of God. You will have the home court advantage.

Reference Section

Prayers

The Prayer of Jabez

Jabez cried out to the God of Israel, "Oh, that you would bless me and enlarge my territory! Let your hand be with me, and keep me from harm so that I will be free from pain." And God granted his request. (1Ch 4:10 NIV)

The Sh'ma

Hear, O Israel: The LORD our God, the LORD is one. Love the LORD your God with all your heart and with all your soul and with all your strength. These commandments that I give you today are to be on your hearts. Impress them on your children. Talk about them when you sit at home and when you walk along the road, when you lie down and when you get up. Tie them as symbols on your hands and bind them on your foreheads. Write them on the doorframes of your houses and on your gates. (Deu 6:4–9 NIV)

The Our Father

"This, then, is how you should pray: "'Our Father in heaven, hallowed be your name, your kingdom come, your will be done, on earth as it is in heaven. Give us today our daily bread. And forgive us our debts, as we also have forgiven our debtors. And lead us not into temptation, but deliver us from the evil one." (Mat 6:9–13 NIV)

Psalm 23:

Psalm 23:1 *A Psalm of David*. The LORD is my shepherd, I shall not want.

He makes me lie down in green pastures; He leads me beside quiet waters.

He restores my soul; He guides me in the paths of righteousness For His name's sake.

Even though I walk through the valley of the shadow of death, I fear no evil; for Thou art with me; Thy rod and Thy staff, they comfort me. Thou dost prepare a table before me in the presence of my enemies; Thou hast anointed my head with oil; My cup overflows. Surely goodness and lovingkindness will follow me all the days of my life, And I will dwell in the house of the LORD forever. (Psa 23:1-6 NAS)

The Ten Commandments

And God spoke all these words: "I am the LORD your God, who brought you out of Egypt, out of the land of slavery. "You shall have no other gods before me. "You shall not make for yourself an image in the form of anything in heaven above or on the earth beneath or in the waters below. You shall not bow down to them or worship them; for I, the LORD your God, am a jealous God, punishing the children for the sin of the parents to the third and fourth generation of those who hate me, but showing love to a thousand generations of those who love me and keep my commandments. "You shall not misuse the name of the LORD your God, for the LORD will not hold anyone guiltless who misuses his name. "Remember the Sabbath day by keeping it holy. Six days you shall labor and do all your work, but the seventh day is a Sabbath to the LORD your God. On it you shall not do any work, neither you, nor your son or daughter, nor your male or female servant, nor your animals, nor any foreigner residing in your towns. For in six days the LORD made the heavens and the earth, the sea, and all that is in them, but he rested on the seventh day. Therefore the LORD blessed the Sabbath day and made it holy. "Honor your father and your mother, so that you may live long in the land the LORD your

God is giving you. "You shall not murder. "You shall not commit adultery. "You shall not steal. "You shall not give false testimony against your neighbor. "You shall not covet your neighbor's house. You shall not covet your neighbor's wife, or his male or female servant, his ox or donkey, or anything that belongs to your neighbor." (Exo 20:1–17 NIV)

Endnotes

---

[1] American Rhetoric: Movie Speech. *The Patriot,* 2000. (http://www.americanrhetoric.com/MovieSpeeches/moviespeechthepatriot.html)

[2] IMDB. "Quotes for Magneto." From X-2, 1999 http://www.imdb.com/character/ch0001128/quotes

[3] IMDB. "Quotes for Morpheus." From *The Matrix. 1999 (http://www.imdb.com/character/ch0000746/quotes)*

[4] Metaxas, Eric. Bonhoeffer: Pastor, Martyr, Prophet, Spy. Nashville: Thomas Nelson Publishing, 2010.

[5] IMDB. "Quotes for Grail Knight." From Indiana Jones and the Last Crusade. 1989 "http://www.imdb.com/title/tt0097576/quotes

[6] "Memorable Quotes by "Marcus Aurelius" (Richard Harris) from *Gladiator. 2000 https://theiapolis.com/movie-0MOL/gladiator/quotes/marcus-aurelius.html*

[7] IMDB. "Sleeper Quotes." 1973 *http://www.imdb.com/title/tt0070707/quotes*

[8] Charles R. Swindoll."Anything Under Gods Control is Never Out of Control". Goodreads. 2014 https://www.goodreads.com/author/quotes/5139.Charles_R_Swindoll

[9] Kaplan, Aryeh. *Maimonides' Principles*. The Fundamentals of Jewish Faith. New York: National Conference of Synagogue, 1975.

[10] IMDB. "Quotes for Morpheus." From *The Matrix. 1999* (*http://www.imdb.com/character/ch0000746/quotes*)

[11] Metaxas, Eric. Bonhoeffer: Pastor, Martyr, Prophet, Spy. Nashville: Thomas Nelson Publishing, 2010.

[12] Metaxas, Eric. Bonhoeffer: Pastor, Martyr, Prophet, Spy. Nashville: Thomas Nelson Publishing, 2010.

[13] Metaxas, Eric. Bonhoeffer: Pastor, Martyr, Prophet, Spy. Nashville: Thomas Nelson Publishing, 2010.

[14] IMDB. "Quotes for Morpheus." From *The Matrix. 1999* (*http://www.imdb.com/character/ch0000746/quotes*)

[15] IMDB. "Quotes for Jerry Maguire." 1996 http://www.imdb.com/title/tt0116695/quotes

[16] *Interview with God. Interviewwithgodsite*. 2010 http://interviewwithgodsite.com/

[17] IMDB. "Quotes for "The Rock." 1996 http://www.imdb.com/title/tt0117500/quotes

[18] "Quotes from the Movie *The American President*." Finest Quotes.com. 1995 http://www.finestquotes.com/movie_quotes/movie/The%20American%20 President/page/0.htm

Bibliography

Frangipane, Francis. *The Three Battle Grounds*. Advancing Church Publications, USA, 1989.

Lewis, C.S. *The Screw Tape Letters*. New York: Macmillan Co., 1943.

Tozer, A. W. *The Knowledge of the Holy*. San Francisco: Harper and Row Publishers, San Francisco, 1961.

Nee, Watchman. *The Spiritual Man*. New York: Christian Fellowship Publisher, Inc., 1968.

Shelly, Bruce L. *Church History in Plain Language*. Dallas: Word Publishing, 1982.

Gruber, Daniel. *The Separation of Church and Faith*. Hanover: Elijah Publishing, 2005.

Gruber, Daniel. The Messianic Writings, Translated and Annotated by Daniel Gruber. Hanover: Elijah Publishing, 2011.

Permissions

G ratitude to Dan Gruber for allowing me to use his life changing work, The Messianic Writings (MW), in a manner that helped achieve the objectives of this book.

CPSIA information can be obtained
at www.ICGtesting.com
Printed in the USA
BVOW06s2026290817

493438BV00008B/21/P

9 781545 611920